How to Sell with a Laptop

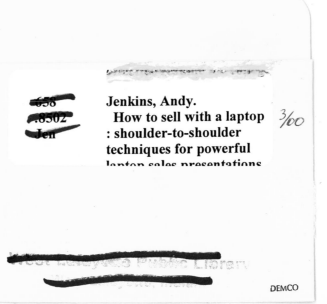

How to Sell with a Laptop

Shoulder-to-Shoulder™ Techniques for Powerful Laptop Sales Presentations

Andy Jenkins
Dick Elder
Dave Thomas

McGraw-Hill
New York   San Francisco   Washington, D.C.   Auckland   Bogotá
Caracas   Lisbon   London   Madrid   Mexico City   Milan
Montreal   New Delhi   San Juan   Singapore
Sydney   Tokyo   Toronto

McGraw-Hill

*A Division of The **McGraw·Hill** Companies*

1 2 3 4 5 6 7 8 9 0   DOC / DOC   9 0 9 8 7 6 5 4 3 2 1 0 9

ISBN 0-07-134521-3   3/00   Davidson 15.26

The sponsoring editor for this book was Richard Narramore, the editing supervisor was Jane Palmieri, the designer was Inkwell Publishing Services, and the production supervisor was Elizabeth J. Strange. It was set in Palatino by Inkwell Publishing Services.

Printed and bound by R.R. Donnelley & Sons Company.

Contents

Chapter 3   Ending the Call   49

Acknowledgments

How to Sell with Your Laptop helps sales professionals turn their laptop computers into the single most powerful sales tool available to them. With a laptop, they can tell their sales story, show sales information, and demonstrate product capabilities in ways never before possible. In writing *How to Sell with a Laptop*, we are privileged to be a part of this critical sales revolution.

Throughout the creation of this book, we have been blessed with a number of people whose knowledge, competence, enthusiasm, and sheer will have made the book possible. We would like to recognize these people, without whose interest and support the effort could not have been accomplished.

First, our customers at TEAM Marketing Group. It is these corporations and their management teams with whom we work who have continued to raise the crossbar of sales competition and innovation that we aspire to achieve and exceed.

Second, we acknowledge the support of the many colleagues in the selling and training industry who have encouraged us at TEAM to develop the book based on our experience living and working in the trenches with thousands of America's best salespeople for more than 25 years.

Every great effort takes a team of people whose target is focused, whose target is measured, and whose target is achieved. Our great team of Cassy Heller, Marci Finkenbinder, Renee Joseph, and a host of contributors are the people whose attention to detail, technical expertise, and constant "push" helped in bringing you this book. One member of our team, however, must be singled out for her outstanding contribution. That person is Carolyn Dunbar, our senior writer and editor. From the beginning of the project, Carolyn has rolled up her sleeves, researched, written, edited, proofed, and touched every page, every sentence, every illustration. Her professionalism, competence, and sheer determination have created a significant impact on *How to Sell with Your Laptop*. For her efforts we are eternally grateful.

And last but not least, we acknowledge our families, who have put up with our crazy schedules throughout the project.

ANDY JENKINS
DICK ELDER
DAVE THOMAS

Introduction

Salespeople live for the next sale. You know this from your own experience. As a salesperson, nothing in your professional life is more challenging, satisfying, or exciting than making the sale—hearing your prospect say, "Yes."

Getting to "yes" is becoming more of a challenge all the time as markets, customers, distribution channels, manufacturers, laboratories, sales managers, product managers, marketers—even accounting departments—demand more out of those of us in the sales profession. Add to those demands the evolution of sales automation (at revolutionary speed!) and you've got the ultimate challenge: blending technology into the most human-interactive of the business professions—*selling*.

How do you sell with a laptop? That's a great question. It's not the same as, "How do you keep up your account information?" or "How do you e-mail someone from a laptop?" or "How do you map your territory?" or "How do you submit your expense reports via computer?"

The question is, "How do you *sell* with your laptop computer?" The answer to that question involves both of the challenges salespeople face: closing the sale and using sales automation effectively.

In this book, you'll find the answer to how to sell with a laptop in a new mode of selling called *Shoulder-to-Shoulder Selling*: positioning the buyer at your shoulder—not across the desk—and allowing you to sell with your laptop or notebook computer!

What Is *Shoulder-to-Shoulder Selling*?

Simply put, *Shoulder-to-Shoulder Selling* is a set of commonsense techniques that will help you use your laptop to maximum effect

as a sales tool to present your products and services. Regardless of what "sales process" you use (consultative selling, strategic selling, etc.), at some point you'll need to explain how your products, services, or ideas can best meet the customer's needs.

When you sell *shoulder-to-shoulder*, you need a presentation that can capture the customer's interest or get your prospect excited about what you have to offer. If you use an interactive multimedia presentation loaded on your laptop, you can:

- Explain the details about your products or services with pictures, audio, video clips, and animations.

- Show examples of how your products can be used in real-life applications.

- Demonstrate the features, benefits, and competitive strengths of your offering (Figure I-1).

- Review technical specs or test results with charts, graphs, and pictures (Figure I-2).

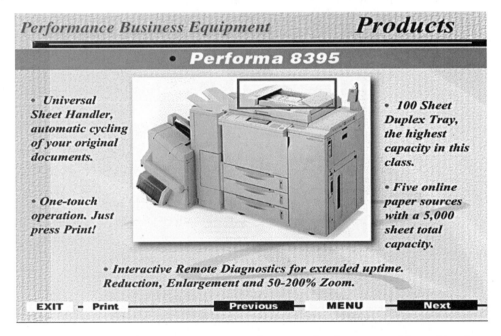

Figure I-1. A well-designed content screen can showcase the features and benefits of your products.

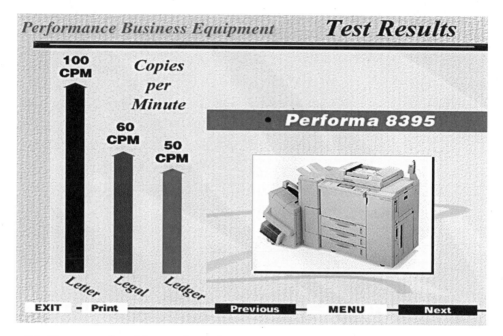

Figure I-2. Use artwork, tables, and graphs to display test results or technical information about your products.

- Share audio or video testimonials from satisfied customers.
- And the list goes on and on!

Best of Both Worlds

In the past, salespeople have typically relied on brochures, overheads, slides, and videos to communicate these details. Today, you can combine the power of all these formats into a single multimedia presentation and never need a slide projector, VCR, or stack of brochures. Now you can use your laptop as the primary sales tool for delivering the message and use printed brochures solely as your "leave-behinds" with customers.

The term *shoulder-to-shoulder* means to eliminate the desk, table, or sales counter as a barrier between you and your prospect or customer. When you sell with your laptop, you sit side-by-side, or *shoulder-to-shoulder*, with your prospect and explore your products in a consultative discussion.

You can use your laptop in many ways to support your sales activity, for example, by:

- *Prospecting for new customers*, using CD-ROM databases and search engines on the Internet.
- *Communicating with customers*, writing letters, sending faxes, and creating proposals.
- *Managing your customer database*, keeping track of your customers and your call activity.
- *Maximizing your time*, using calendar programs for scheduling appointments.
- *Communicating with the home office*, downloading new information, sending letters/expense reports, and checking on order status and product availability.

Maximize Face Time

All of these are important uses for your laptop, and you will find some of these activities explained here, but they are not the focus of this book. *How to Sell with a Laptop* concentrates on how to maximize the most important asset you have—"face time" with customers! That's where your laptop can best help you accelerate your sales process.

What's in It for Me?

The "old school" of veteran salespeople can produce many reasons why they don't use a laptop in front of customers. Do these sound familiar?

"I can use a brochure and explain it faster by myself."

"I don't like computers. I'm not comfortable with how to use them."

"I can't find the information and don't want to look foolish in front of my customer."

"Computers aren't dependable. I'd rather rely on myself."

"I have my own unique style of selling that doesn't lend itself to using a computer."

"My customers are low-tech. They would be offended if I used a computer during the call."

"I'm already successful without it. Why should I change?"

Perception is reality. It's true. If you're not confident and comfortable during the sales call, your chances for success are greatly reduced. Change is difficult and often resisted. If you're convinced that you can't sell with a laptop, then you will probably fail.

Maybe you've never had anyone show you how to sell with your laptop. Maybe you've never seen the look on a customer's face when he or she watches a fun, interactive presentation. Or maybe you're like the majority of sales reps who received a laptop, an owner's manual, and a brief introduction on how to communicate with the home office. No one has really trained them on how to create a basic sales presentation or use it in front of a customer.

The bottom line is simple: As salespeople, we can be the most perceptive, open-minded people in the world if we see a reason to change. If we see value in using a new tool that will help us sell more, we'll try it . . . once. But we'd better have a positive first experience right off, or we'll never try it again.

That's why we created *How to Sell with a Laptop*. We've taken years of experience in selling with a laptop and boiled it all down into a series of *best practices* so you can feel more comfortable and confident the very first time you try it. We know that it works; we've done it ourselves, and we've seen the results.

To keep it simple, we've boiled down hundreds of reasons why you should sell with a laptop into five main benefits for you.

1. Selling with a Laptop Accelerates Your Sales Process!

Multimedia presentations consistently get people more excited and generate more interest than static brochures or overhead presentations. Laptop presentations combine the best of all worlds— sight, sound, motion, and graphics—coupled with your valuable presentation skills.

The results are clear: You will accelerate the sale if you can visually demonstrate and verbally explain why your products/services are exactly what the customer needs to solve his or her problems!

2. Selling with a Laptop Makes You Look Great!

When you know your presentation, you can quickly answer questions and objections with more than just your verbal skills. When customers can see it (visually) and hear it (verbally from you), they will feel more comfortable with your response.

Another advantage—you can stop worrying about memorizing every detail and specification. Let the computer be the keeper of the knowledge while you master using the knowledge. Your laptop allows you to stay focused on understanding the customer's needs (qualifying) and to visually demonstrate how your products/services can solve customer problems.

When you learn how to master your laptop to visually impress your customers, your professionalism and expertise will be truly enhanced. Showmanship still plays an important part in your sales success, and good laptop skills will definitely improve your showmanship and style.

3. Selling with a Laptop Saves Time and Money

How many times have you found yourself in front of a decision maker without the brochure, product sample, or data page you need at your fingertips? You left it in the car or back at the office.

When you sell with your laptop, you will have ready access to all your product information, features and benefits, spec sheets, test results—and even your brochures—*during* your sales call! You don't have to worry about forgetting support material. Everything is always with you. Just open your laptop and show the decision maker exactly what he or she needs to see—right now!

4. Selling with a Laptop Keeps You in Control

With your laptop, you control what the customer sees and when you want the customer to see it. You choose the approach and content screens that best support your sales approach.

Conversely, when you sell with a brochure, invariably your customer picks it up and starts paging through it. Now he or she is in control, and you're reacting to the customer's quick-scan approach to reviewing your product line.

With your laptop, you're sitting side-by-side in a consultative discussion. The desk is no longer between you and your customer. It's amazing how this *shoulder-to-shoulder* seating arrangement will change the dynamics of your sales call.

5. Selling with Your Laptop Maximizes Your Face Time

Time with a decision maker is your most valuable asset. A laptop will help you maximize the face time with your customer. You can show product information using video clips, animations, and graphics—all without bringing the physical product with you on the call.

When used correctly, a laptop computer will enhance your overall sales professionalism. With what you can show on a laptop, you stand a better chance of impressing the decision maker, and as a result, your chances for success will skyrocket.

How Is Laptop Selling Different?

It's good to remember that a laptop cannot substitute for good interpersonal sales skills. What are some of those basic sales skills? Here's a partial list, for starters:

- Alertness to the selling environment
- Sensitivity to verbal and nonverbal cues—alertness to body language
- The right blend of courtesy and assertiveness
- Good listening skills—questioning, listening, responding
- Preparedness
- Thorough product knowledge
- Knowledge of your marketplace and your competition
- Personal confidence
- The ability to accurately qualify your prospects so you don't waste your time or theirs
- Solution-oriented, problem-solving attitude
- Customer-service orientation

- The ability to control the call to your advantage
- Excellent and immediate follow-through on customer requests

These are sales fundamentals you're probably bringing to your sales call already. In that sense, selling with a laptop computer is no different from the way you have been selling for years. Now, however, you have a powerful tool that, when used properly, can give you an even more powerful edge during a sales call.

And yet *selling with a laptop is different in three basic ways*, depending on the experience of the salesperson who uses it:

1. Some salespeople have never touched a laptop computer—or any computer.

2. Other salespeople are familiar with computers and may use a laptop for other aspects of selling, but they haven't yet used it during a sales call.

3. Many road warriors are veteran laptop presenters, but may not be aware of some commonsense techniques that will help them to use the system more effectively and get to the bottom line more quickly.

Let's take a look at each case.

Salespeople Who Have Never Touched a Laptop. The biggest difference starts with embracing change. If you have never used a laptop, you may be apprehensive about the technology. The difference between the way you sold before and how you'll sell now comes in your willingness to invest the time to learn to use and trust the system. By investing that time, you'll become confident in front of customers.

The good news is that by studying *How to Sell with a Laptop*, you have already taken a major step forward in conquering the technology. In fact, the Appendix of this book is called "Laptop 101 for New Users." It gives simple instructions that show you step-by-step how to start your computer, load a program, run a program, create a shortcut for that program, manage your power supply, access the Internet, fax a document from your laptop, and perform many other basic tasks you need to master as you use your laptop to sell.

Practice makes perfect. Practice also makes for comfort and confidence. By practicing with your laptop—and by using the hands-on exercises suggested at the end of each chapter—you will begin to recognize the power of the tool itself and the efficiencies it can bring to your daily activities.

One big change for those who have never touched a laptop is to become accustomed to taking it on the road. At anywhere from 9 to 11 pounds, a laptop is heavy when you're lugging it through the airport. On the bright side, manufacturers are making portables lighter than ever before. And a laptop is already far lighter than a sample case. Plus the durable "briefcases-on-wheels" carry-ons you can find everywhere today will minimize actual lifting and carrying during your trip.

Salespeople Who Are Familiar with Computers, but Have Never Used a Laptop during a Sales Call. The difference is in learning to present sales information effectively. If you are already using a computer in your work life, your comfort level is pretty high, which gives you an advantage up front. The challenge comes in beginning to think differently about what the laptop means to your earning power.

Consider the big distinction between using your laptop to stay connected with customers (tracking sales information, creating proposals, writing letters, or faxing documents) and actually using your laptop to present sales information during a sales call. Although the preparation and follow-up steps are certainly important—and this book looks at these steps in great detail (see Chapters 1 and 3)—it's the *shoulder-to-shoulder* time with your customer that is your best chance to present yourself, your company, and your company's products and services in person. It's your strongest opportunity to generate revenue.

As a computer user, you may have mastered the benefits of sales force automation software, you may depend on e-mail every day to stay in touch with clients, and you may be terrific at spinning out letters and proposals. You'll need a different mind-set, though—and perhaps a leap of faith—to consider your laptop as your primary sales tool for getting to the bottom line faster and more efficiently when you're *shoulder-to-shoulder* with your prospects and customers.

It's easy to fall into the trap of believing that working on the computer is the same as selling. For the already-computer-literate salesperson, this represents the main difference and the toughest challenge in the way you do business.

As a computer-savvy salesperson, you can do many things right away to begin the transition to *selling* with a laptop, including learning to make a basic PowerPoint presentation. You can begin to collect sales information, cost-comparison charts, price sheets, spec sheets, feature/benefits tables, and many other support materials on your laptop and organize them so that they're accessible in an instant when you need them during a call.

How to Sell with a Laptop will cover these and many other techniques and strategies in detail.

What about Veteran Laptop Presenters? What is the difference for an experienced road warrior? *Shoulder-to-Shoulder Selling* techniques can help you become smarter, more aware, and more effective during your sales calls. You will learn when to transition to your laptop, how to involve your customer in your laptop presentation, and how to prevent the laptop from becoming the sole focus of the call. You will also learn how to structure your presentations to include logical breaks where you can ask key qualifying questions, helping your customer advance in the decision-making process.

Even salespeople in technology fields, who have been using their laptops for years to showcase their software or product capabilities on-screen, may not have the skills they need to present information effectively. Their ability to speak in technical jargon does not automatically translate to the ability to deliver a persuasive sales presentation. But with powerful material, powerful salesmanship, and powerful presentation skills, the veteran laptop presenter has a much better chance of getting to "yes."

How to Use This Book

How to Sell with a Laptop is really a fun, self-study course you can take at your own pace. Each chapter is followed by a set of simple exercises. These are designed to familiarize you with the functions of your system and to give you opportunities to create a presentation and practice delivering it with your laptop.

The end of each chapter also features a section on how to avoid pitfalls. These "real-life" pitfalls are the result of all-too-vivid experience in what not to do with your laptop in a sales situation. They may allow you to avoid mistakes by helping you *not* to go where others have gone before!

For New Laptop Users

If you are a new laptop user, start by reading Chapters 1 and 2 in Part 1, "How to Sell with Your Laptop." Then jump to the Appendix at the back of the book, "Laptop 101 for New Users." Read the simple steps in the Appendix that will get you started using your laptop.

Next read Chapter 11, "Traveling with Your Laptop," for some good tips on how to back up your documents, maintain your system, and manage power and batteries. You'll also find general tips about traveling and hooking up your system when you're on the road.

Return to finish Part 1 by reading Chapters 3 and 4. Next, complete Parts 2, 3, and 4 by reading Chapters 5 through 10. At your leisure, take advantage of practice opportunities by completing the exercises at the end of each chapter.

For Experienced Laptop Users

First, read through Part 1, "How to Sell with Your Laptop," and complete the exercises following Chapters 1 through 4. Next, read Part 2, "Creating Powerful Presentations." Practice creating your own basic presentation in PowerPoint. Then review Part 3, "Laptop Logistics," and Part 4, "User Tips and Tools." Refer to the Appendix, "Laptop 101 for New Users," as needed to refresh your memory about using your laptop system.

Take the book at your own pace, and use the sections of the book that are most relevant to your sales activities.

Ten Key Ideas on Selling with Your Laptop

Of the many ideas and techniques presented in this book, here are 10 key ideas to consider.

1. *Buy the best equipment you can afford.* All the new laptops, notebooks, and portables offer CD-ROM drives. If your current laptop does not have a CD-ROM drive, trade up.

2. *Review as many computer-based sales presentations as you can get your hands on to learn what is possible to show on your laptop.* Be aware of what's out on the market. Find a way to get access to your competitor's computer-based presentation as a basis of comparison.

3. *Practice your sales presentation with your laptop—both by yourself and among friends and associates who can give you constructive feedback.* Practice will help you overcome any apprehension you may feel.

4. *Load your frequently used sales support materials (spec sheets, feature/benefit charts, cost-comparison charts, "pencil-sell" worksheets, price lists, product photos) onto your laptop and learn how to organize them so you can access them quickly during a sales call.* This is one of the most powerful sales techniques you can use to your advantage with your laptop.

5. *Learn to send a nonverbal signal that you intend to use your laptop during the call.* Take your laptop out of the case and carry it under your left arm as you walk into the call.

6. *Just before the call, boot up your system, launch your presentation, and then put your laptop into **Suspend** mode.* When you're ready to present your sales information during the call, you won't have to wait for the system to boot up. With the touch of a button, you're ready to go!

7. *Establish rapport with your customer or prospect first, before opening your laptop.* Avoid the temptation to turn to it too soon.

8. *Let your laptop presentation do its job, but use body language and verbal cues to stay in control of your sales call.*

9. *Control the lighting so your presentation can be seen.* Failure to do this simple step is an all-too-common mistake salespeople make. Be sure to situate the laptop away from sources of glare.

10. *The most powerful concept in selling with a laptop computer is to move your customer into a position next to you*—shoulder-to-shoulder—*so you are both looking together at your sales information.* Now you're both on the same side of the table or "barrier"; you have overcome the "adversarial" posture of sitting opposite your customer with a desk between you. You're now working together to discover solutions to your customer's problems!

If all you take away from *How to Sell with a Laptop* are these 10 key points, you'll already be ahead of the game.

Come on—relax and enjoy the rest of the book. Have fun with it! You're already well on your way to mastering the simple *Shoulder-to-Shoulder Selling* techniques that will help you use your laptop computer to gain an edge over your competition and win more business!

• Part 1 •

How to Sell with Your Laptop

• CHAPTER 1 •

Preparing for the Call

For the moment, let's assume that you have made your own basic presentation, or that your marketing department (or someone else) has created one for you. (Later in Chapters 5, 6, and 7, you'll learn some great tips for designing your own sales presentation.) Let's also assume you have a laptop with either of three operating systems: Windows 95, Windows 98, or Windows NT. We'll further assume that you know how to turn on your laptop and use the pointing device (touchpad, trackball, eraser head, mouse, etc.). Another assumption is that you have Microsoft PowerPoint or equivalent presentation software.

Note: If you'd like more information on your Windows laptop, please turn to the Appendix, "Laptop 101 for New Users." Also, whenever you see step-by-step instructions on how to perform a certain laptop task, you will find these steps provided for all three operating systems (Windows 95, Windows 98, and Windows NT). Words that refer to items on the systems are shown in boldface type.

Aside from all the things you normally do to prepare for a call, you'll need to complete these five tasks to maximize your success:

1. Load your presentation (if made by someone else) and make sure it works on your laptop.

2. Practice your presentation so you know how to find key content.

3. Customize the initial screen with your prospect's name (if you're using a basic presentation like a PowerPoint presentation).

4. Make a **Shortcut** on your **Desktop** screen to easily launch your presentation.

5. Make sure the laptop battery is fully charged.

Step 1: Load Your Presentation

Load your presentation (if made by someone else) and make sure it works on your laptop. If you receive a show on a single diskette, here's how easy it is to copy it onto your hard drive using Windows 95:

- First, double-click on **My Computer**; double-click on your hard disk drive, typically your **C-drive**; then create a new folder and name it something like "Presentations" (**File**, **New**, **Folder**, type "Presentations") (Figure 1-1).

- Close all open windows.

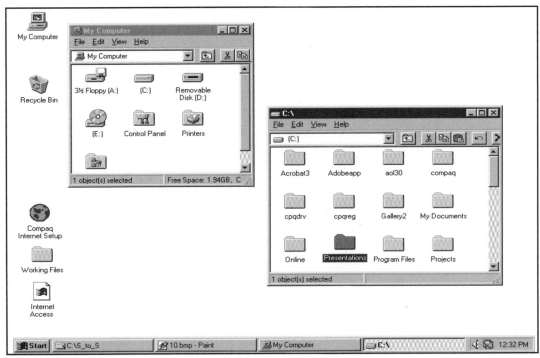

Figure 1-1. Create a new folder named "Presentations."

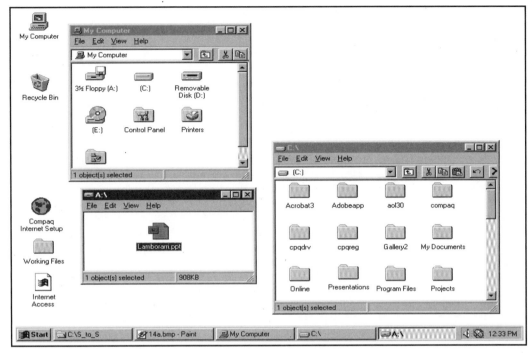

Figure 1-2. Insert the diskette and open your floppy drive.

- Next, insert your diskette, and double-click on **My Computer**; from the **My Computer** window, double-click on your floppy drive, typically the **A-drive** (Figure 1-2).

- Next, drag and drop the file from the diskette onto the new folder on your **C-drive** and it will be automatically copied for your use (Figure 1-3). It's that easy!

- To play the presentation, just double-click on the new file on your **C-drive**, and it should launch, assuming you have the software it was created with. Then you can click through the various content screens and make sure everything looks OK on your laptop screen (Figure 1-4).

Note: In PowerPoint, to view all the "slides" in the show, click on the "double down arrow" in the lower right part of the screen to advance to the next slide.

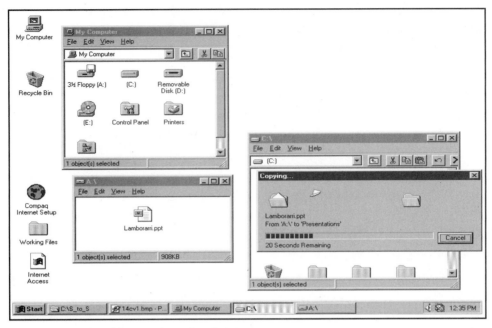

Figure 1-3. Copying a file onto your hard drive.

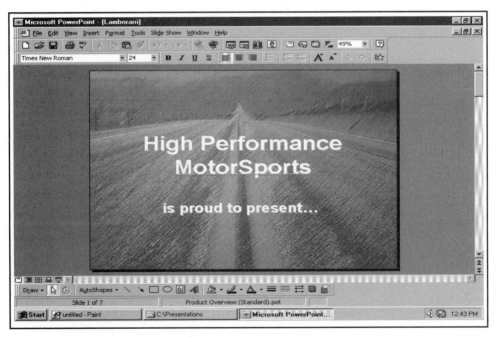

Figure 1-4. Example of a presentation in PowerPoint.

Loading and Playing Single-Disk Presentations	
Windows 98 Instructions	*Windows NT Instructions*
Insert the presentation diskette into your **A-drive**.	Insert the presentation diskette into your **A-drive**.
Double-click on **My Computer**, and then double-click on **A-drive**.	Double-click on **My Computer**, and then double-click on **A-drive**.
Drag the presentation icon onto the **Desktop** and drop it.	Drag the presentation icon onto the **Desktop** and drop it.
Close all open windows.	In Windows NT, this action will also launch the presentation.

Loading and Playing Multidisk Presentations

With a lot of multimedia shows, the file size can exceed what will fit on one disk. Developers will typically use an installation program to make it easy to load. Follow these simple instructions for Windows 95:

- Insert Disk 1 into your laptop.

- Click on **Start**, go to **Settings**, and choose **Control Panel** (Figure 1-5).

- Double-click on **Add/Remove Programs** (Figure 1-6).

- Click on **Install** (Figure 1-7). The system will find the setup file and ask you a few questions. This is called a *wizard*.

- Pay close attention to the location where the file will be installed so you can find it later to launch the presentation.

- Follow the prompts when the system asks you to insert additional disks. You're on your way to loading the presentation!

- To play this type of presentation, once again, find and open the folder where your presentation is located (on your **C-drive**) and double-click on the file to play it. Look for files with the ending ".exe." These will typically be the files to double-click on to play advanced presentations (Figure 1-8).

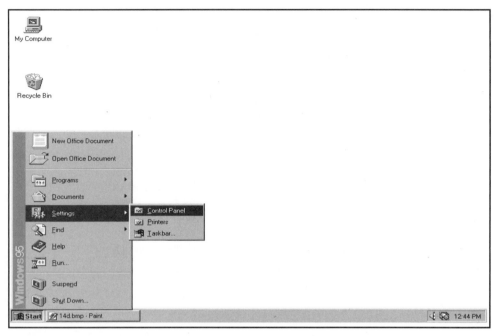

Figure 1-5. Reach **Control Panel** from the **Start** button.

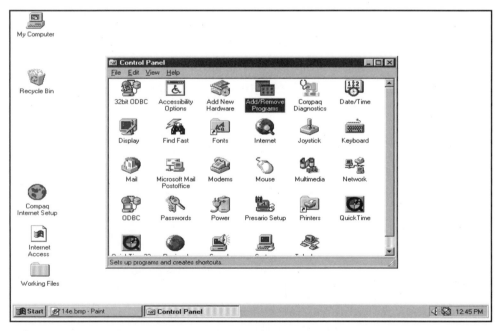

Figure 1-6. Double-click on **Add/Remove Programs** in the **Control Panel**.

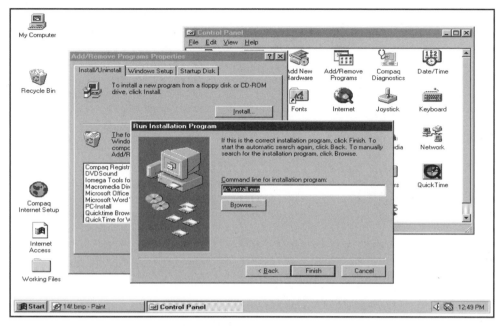

Figure 1-7. Installing multidisk presentations.

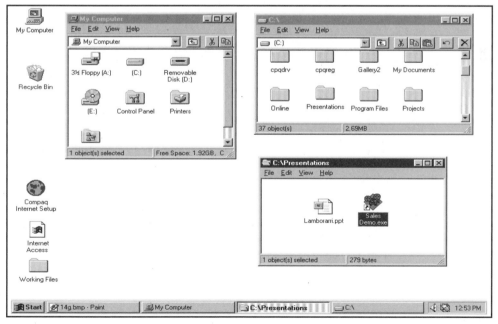

Figure 1-8. Launch your presentation by double-clicking the file (typically ending with ".exe").

- A quicker way to play the presentation—once it has been installed—is to go to the **Start** button, select the **Programs** menu, and find the presentation file. Select it to launch and play.

Loading and Playing Multidisk Presentations

Note: Windows 95, Windows 98, and Windows NT are the same for this function.

Insert Disk 1 into the **A-drive**.

Click on **Start**, go to **Settings**, and choose **Control Panel**.

Next, double-click on **Add/Remove Programs**.

Then click on **Install**. If the computer finds the program file, it will ask you a few questions, to which you will answer **Next** until **Finish**.

The dialog boxes are called *wizards*.

You may need to browse the **A-drive** to find your program file. It will usually be under the word *Setup* or *Install*.

Then follow the prompts when the system asks you to insert additional disks.

Once the program is installed, you will be able to find that presentation from the **Start**, **Programs** menu to find the proper folder and program to run.

Loading and Playing CD-ROM Presentations

With some CD-ROM presentations, you may need to load a small part of the file for it to play. With others, you can play them directly from the CD-ROM. Follow these simple Windows 95 instructions:

- Begin by reading the instructions on the CD-ROM or the back of the case to see what is required.

- After inserting the CD, it's also a good idea to double-click on the "Read Me" file (on the CD-ROM) to read it first (Figure 1-9).

- To load the presentation, go to **Start**, then **Settings**, then **Control Panel** (Figure 1-10).

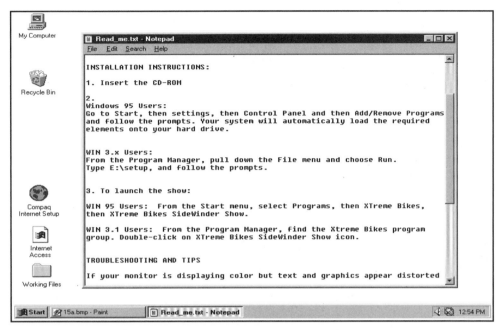

Figure 1-9. "Read Me" file.

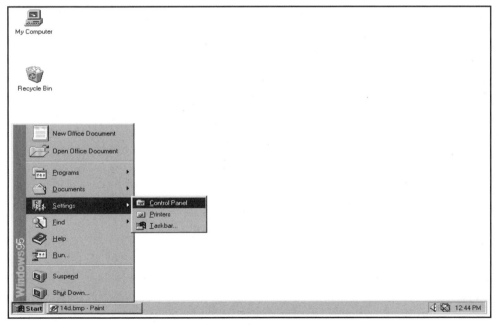

Figure 1-10. Loading a CD-ROM.

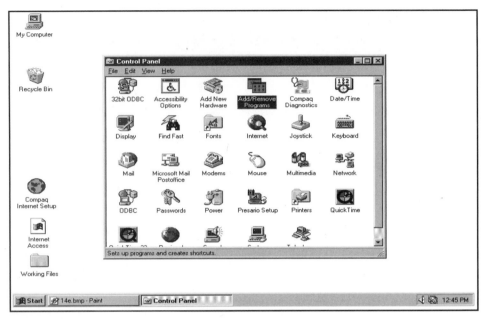

Figure 1-11. Double-click on **Add/Remove Programs** in the **Control Panel** window.

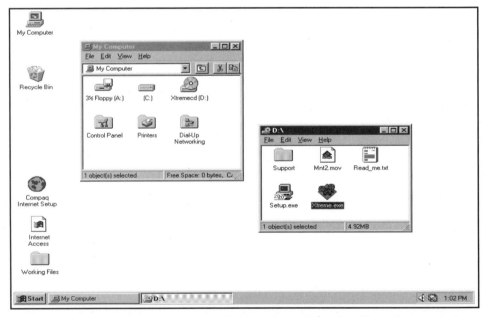

Figure 1-12. Play a CD-ROM presentation by double-clicking the file ending with ".exe."

- Then double-click on **Add/Remove Programs** and **Install** and follow the prompts. Your system will automatically load the required elements onto your hard drive (Figure 1-11).

- To play a CD-ROM presentation (after it's installed), one technique is to open **My Computer**, and then double-click on the CD-ROM drive to view the files on the CD-ROM. Once again, look for a file with an ".exe" on the end and double-click on it to play the presentation (Figure 1-12). You can control your audio level and screen brightness to make it look sharp and adjust the sound to the appropriate level for your presentation.

Loading and Playing CD-ROM Presentations

Note: Windows 95, Windows 98, and Windows NT are the same for this function.

These steps are basically the same as for Loading and Playing Multidisk Presentations.

Insert the CD-ROM into your laptop.

Click on **Start**, go to **Settings**, and choose **Control Panel**.

Next, double-click on **Add/Remove Programs**.

Then click on **Install**. If the computer finds the program file, it will ask you a few questions, to which you will answer **Next** until **Finish**.

Once the program is installed, you will be able to find that presentation from the **Start**, **Programs** menu to find the proper folder and program to run.

No matter which operating system you're using, your laptop system offers several options on how to load and play a show. Feel free to use your own preferred method or follow the easy steps we have reviewed in this section.

Step 2. Practice Your Presentation

Practice your presentation so you know how to find key content. If you don't know your presentation—inside and out—you're dead in the water. Most customers won't be patient very long if you're not prepared. The goal is to be able to find answers to common questions in two or three clicks. Try these practice techniques.

- For basic linear presentations, just click from slide to slide through the show and memorize the flow (Figure 1-13).

- For advanced multimedia presentations, think of the presentation as a family tree. Try each "branch" and learn where it goes. Practice using the navigation buttons on the main menu and submenus to see where they take you (Figure 1-14).

- If necessary, write down exactly how to locate the key content screens you'll use most until you're comfortable in finding them quickly.

- Another good practice technique is to review your presentation right before you walk in the customer's door, just to refresh your memory and prepare for the call.

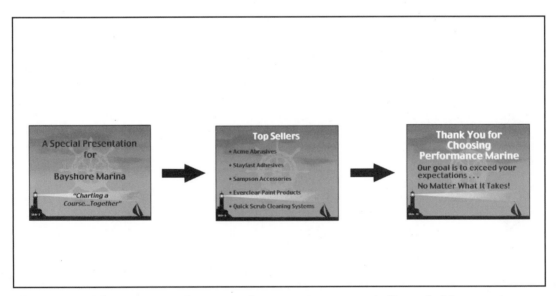

Figure 1-13. A basic presentation moves from screen to screen in linear fashion.

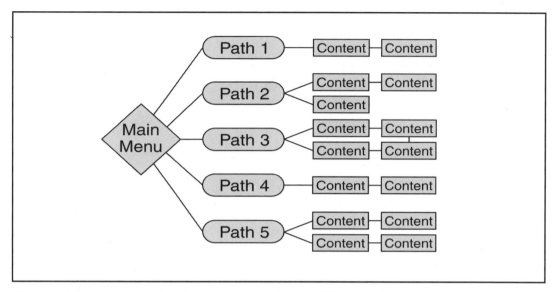

Figure 1-14. An advanced presentation branches out like a family tree.

Step 3. Customize Your Basic Presentation

Customize the initial screen of a basic presentation with your prospect's name—it's easy and impressive. Follow these simple steps for PowerPoint in Windows 95, Windows 98, or Windows NT:

- First, open your PowerPoint presentation from your **C-drive** (Figure 1-15).

- Go to **Insert** and select **New Slide**. Choose an auto layout that includes a box for text (Figure 1-16).

- Then click on the text box and type "A Special Presentation for Mr. Bob Thomas" and adjust it for size and position (Figure 1-17).

- Go to **Slide Sorter View** (slides will be small) and move this new slide to the front of the show (Figure 1-18). Add a transition to the second slide, save the file by typing the keyboard command **[Ctrl] + [S]**, and you're done.

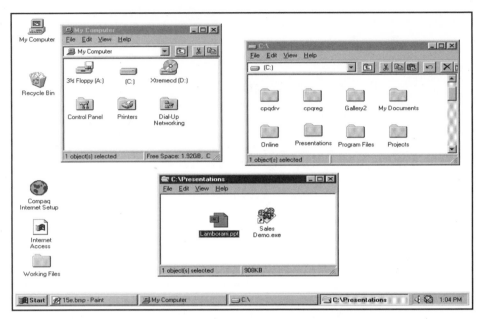

Figure 1-15. Find your basic presentation on the **C-drive** and double-click the file to open it.

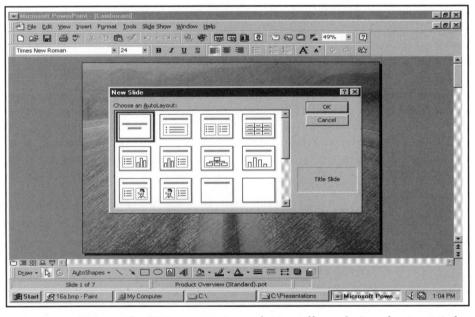

Figure 1-16. PowerPoint and other presentation software offer a choice of automatic layout options.

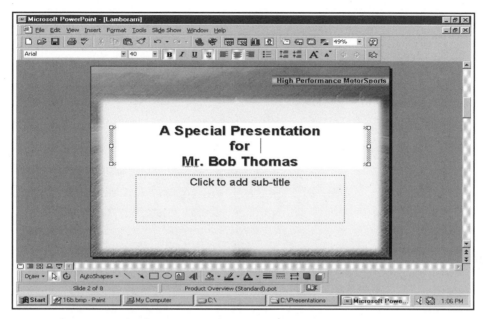

Figure 1-17. Customize the first screen of a basic presentation.

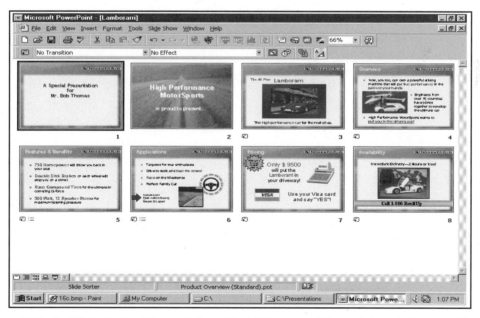

Figure 1-18. In **Slide Sorter View** click and hold the new slide and drag it into position at the top of the show (top left).

Now when you launch your presentation in **Slide Show View**, your customer's name will be prominently displayed on the screen.

Step 4. Make *Shortcuts* to Launch Your Presentation

Make a **Shortcut** for quick access to easily launch your presentation. Making a **Shortcut** allows you to launch presentations from your **Desktop**. This saves time and makes you look professional when you do this during a sales call.

Let's assume you have four different presentations you like to use—for example, a product presentation, a cost-comparison worksheet, technical specs, and customer testimonials. Rather than search on your **C-drive** to find four separate presentations when you're in front of the customer, make a **Shortcut** to each one and put these **Shortcuts** on your **Desktop**. Follow these Windows 95 instructions:

- Open **My Computer** and then your **C-drive** and find your first presentation. Click on it once to select it (Figure 1-19).

- Then go to the **File** menu and choose **Create Shortcut**. Drag the **Shortcut** onto your **Desktop**, and you're done (Figure 1-20).

- Do the same thing with your other three presentations; then close your **C-drive** and **My Computer** windows.

From now on, whenever you want to launch one of these shows, simply double-click on your **Desktop Shortcut** and your presentation will launch.

Making a *Shortcut* on Your Desktop

Note: Windows 95, Windows 98, and Windows NT are the same for this function.

Find the presentation file. Select it and drag it with the right mouse button to the **Desktop**.

A **Shortcut** menu will appear.

Select **Create a Shortcut** here.

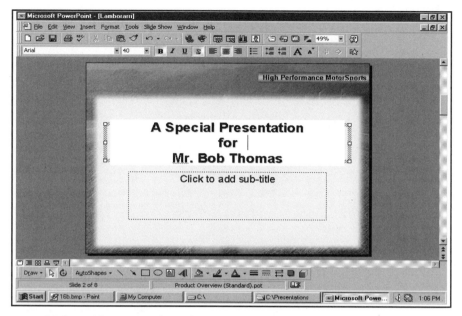

Figure 1-19. Make a **Shortcut** to launch your presentation.

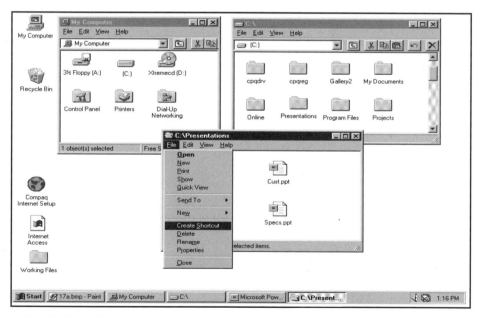

Figure 1-20. Making **Shortcut** icons.

Step 5. Keep Your Laptop Batteries Charged

Make sure your laptop battery is fully charged. Read your instruction manual about how to check the battery level on your particular system. Some models require that the battery be fully discharged before it can recharge properly.

For most laptops all you need to do is plug in your laptop every night to make sure your battery is fully charged. The system can be turned off, and the battery will still recharge provided the laptop is plugged in. If you use your laptop a lot during the day, keep your power cord and an extension cord with you in case you need to "plug in" during the call.

Summary

In this chapter you have learned five commonsense steps that will help prepare you to make a *shoulder-to-shoulder* sales call using your laptop computer. By far, the most important of these steps is to practice your presentation. The more you practice, the more comfortable you will be with customers. When you're comfortable, you're more relaxed and more free to focus on advancing your sales process.

How to Avoid the Pitfalls in Preparing for the Call	
Pitfall	*Try This*
I can't locate the "executable" file for my presentation after I've loaded it onto my laptop.	• When loading the presentation, pay careful attention to the folder name to which your operating system copies the presentation. Write it down. Also write down the name of the presentation file.
	• Go to the **Start** button and choose **Find**. Select **Files and Folders**. In the dialog box, type in part or all of a filename to search. The system will find all similar filenames and show you which folder to look in.
	• After you load your presentation, follow the instructions in this chapter on making a **Shortcut** icon on your **Desktop** so you can easily find your presentation.

How to Avoid the Pitfalls in Preparing for the Call (*Cont.*)

Pitfall	*Try This*
Sometimes I don't remember where the facts and figures I use most often are located within my advanced presentation.	• On a small "sticky" note, write down the sequence of "clicks" that will take you to the appropriate information. • Tape the note next to the trackpad on your laptop, so you'll have it whenever you need it. • Or use the **Notepad** or **Stickies** application (accessed from the **Start** button; choose **Programs** and then **Accessories**) to write a "sticky" note that will appear on your **Desktop** every time you launch the system. During a call, **Minimize** your presentation to the **Taskbar** so you can read your "sticky" note reminder whenever you need it. • Practice with your presentation—clicking every navigation button over and over—until you are comfortable in clicking to every critical piece of information in the show. • Better yet, take the time to memorize your presentation backward and forward.
I customized my basic presentation for Mr. Jones but forgot to change this screen before calling on Ms. Smith. It was embarrassing.	• Boot your laptop and launch your basic presentation before every call. • Check the first screen, and make any necessary corrections. • Then put the laptop on **Suspend**, and you're ready!
My laptop went dead in the middle of my last presentation. I thought the battery had been fully charged.	• Keep your power cord with you at all times. Use the cord rather than relying on battery power if you anticipate your presentation will be lengthy. • Plug your laptop in overnight, every night. • Check with your dealer or local computer store for an adapter for your car cigarette lighter. When you're driving, plug in the laptop and keep the battery charged. • Reread the battery charging instructions in your user's manual. On some models, the battery must be completely discharged before it can take a full charge again.

Practical Exercises

Exercise 1-1. If you've never loaded a presentation onto your laptop, try using the various options outlined in this chapter. Go to the **Start** button and select in this order:

- **Settings**
- **Control Panel**
- **Add/Remove Programs**

Get familiar with this window. If you have a presentation from your company, try loading it onto your laptop.

Exercise 1-2. Practice customizing the first screen of a basic presentation.

Exercise 1-3. Practice making **Shortcuts** and placing them on your **Desktop**. Open **My Computer** and pick any presentation or document. Create a **Shortcut** for it. Try opening your presentation from the new **Shortcut**.

Exercise 1-4. Practice using PowerPoint (or whatever presentation software you have) so you understand how to:

- Move back and forth from the "working" view to a full-screen **Slide Show View**.
- Modify the content in "working" or **Slide View**.
- Advance to the next screen (slide).
- Back up to previous screens (slides).

• CHAPTER 2 •

Shoulder-to-Shoulder Techniques for Presenting with Your Laptop

Consider using the following *shoulder-to-shoulder* techniques (SSTs) when using your laptop to explain your products, services, and/or ideas.

SST-1—Use *Suspend* to Save Time

One of the handiest tips you can use on a sales call is to start your laptop, let it boot up, and then put it to **Sleep** or **Suspend** it just before you walk in the door for your appointment.

The main benefit is to avoid the time-consuming start-up process your laptop goes through just to get to your **Desktop** screen. If you use this **Suspend** technique, you'll be up and running in less than half the time it would otherwise take. It's simple to do with Windows 95. Go to **Start**, choose **Suspend**, and you're done! (Figure 2-1)

Keep in mind, every laptop is a little different when it comes to waking up. Some have a button to push, and on others, you may have to push the main power switch. It's best to read your owner's manual on **Suspend** to see how to wake up your laptop.

Set Laptop to *Suspend* or *Sleep*	
Windows 98 Instructions	*Windows NT Instructions*
From the **Start** button select **Shut Down**. Then click **Standby**. Consult your hardware user's manual for how to wake up the system.	Windows NT does *not* offer a **Suspend** option from the **Start** button. You can only **Shut Down** and then confirm in the dialog box whether you really want to **Shut Down** or **Restart**. Consult your hardware user's manual for specifics on how to **Suspend** and wake up your system.

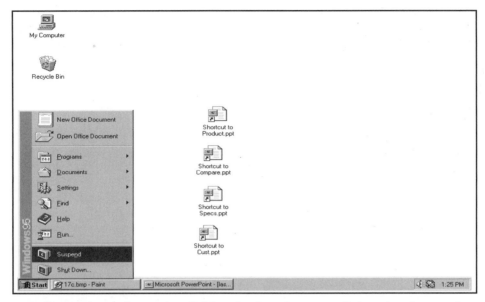

Figure 2-1. Suspend your laptop by clicking the **Start** button and choosing **Suspend**.

SST-2—Launch Your Show before the Call

Another good tip is to launch your show out in the car, hallway, lobby, or waiting area—even the rest room!—then set your laptop to **Sleep** or **Suspend**. That way your sales presentation will already be up and running when you "wake up" your laptop.

If you have a favorite screen or place within your basic or advanced presentation, you can launch your show, find that spot, and then **Suspend** your laptop. When you're ready to transition to your laptop later during your sales call, the information you need will already be on-screen.

SST-3—Send a Nonverbal Signal That You Intend to Use Your Laptop

As you greet your prospect, carry your laptop under your left arm so you can easily shake hands. This sends a nonverbal signal that you have brought your laptop and intend to use it. This simple nonverbal signal helps prepare your customer to see the information you have to show.

SST-4—Observe Your Selling Environment

Check out your selling environment right away for windows and overhead light sources that may cause a glare problem on your screen. Obviously, your customer cannot be interested in or impressed by what you have to present if he or she cannot see what's on your laptop screen.

The goal is to point your laptop screen away from glare-producing light sources to maximize its readability for you and your customer. If possible, adjust the lighting in the room, close the drapes or blinds, dim the overhead lights, or do whatever is necessary to ensure screen readability. This is a commonsense step, but it's often overlooked.

In some cases, it will be impossible to change the lighting in your selling environment. When that happens, simply be sure to adjust the angle of the laptop screen and swivel it to face your customer directly. Ask if he or she can see the screen. If necessary, adjust the screen contrast and brightness.

SST-5—Choose a Good Selling Location

You'll sell *shoulder-to-shoulder* more effectively if you can eliminate the barrier of the desk between you and your customer.

As you are walking in the door for your sales appointment, look for a neutral selling location, such as a table or credenza, where you can set up your laptop when the right time comes. If a table or credenza isn't available, consider using the customer's desk. Pick a location where light from windows won't be a problem.

If possible, put your laptop directly in front of the customer so he or she doesn't have to move. If you can't get your chair next to the customer, kneel down so you're at eye level.

Optional alternative: Ask if you can move to a conference room or spare office (that's not currently in use). This is perfectly acceptable and may be your best bet.

SST-6—Don't Use Your Laptop Too Soon

Don't jump the gun. Avoid the mistake of using your laptop too early in the call. It's important to let the customer get comfortable with you first. In fact, it's critical to your success that you complete the initial steps of a consultative sales process before you use your laptop. Fully qualify the customer's needs and concerns. Make sure you've established rapport and demonstrated your own expertise.

In some cases, you may not even use your laptop on an initial call—and that's OK. Remember, your laptop is part of presenting your solutions; it's not the main focus of your sales call.

Try these techniques to build your own credibility before you use your laptop: Look the customer in the eye. Sell him or her on your own expertise. Use your interpersonal skills to qualify the customer and understand any needs or concerns.

SST-7—Use a Simple Transition to Your Laptop

When the timing is right, use a simple transition like, "Based on what you've told me, let me show you an interactive presentation that will demonstrate how we can meet your needs and concerns." Then, don't hesitate. Open your laptop and begin the wake-up process. Stand up and carry it to your preselected neutral location. The key is to stay in control. You don't need to ask for permission.

SST-8—Set the Stage for Your Presentation

Now that your customer is sitting next to you, launch your presentation by double-clicking on the **Shortcut** you've made on your **Desktop** screen. As your presentation is launching, verbally set the stage for what your customer is about to see. Briefly summarize the information you will show. This will prevent your customer from feeling intimidated by what may look like a lengthy show.

SST-9—Don't Talk as Your Introduction Runs

Listen quietly as you let your opening segment do its job. If you're using an advanced presentation that has music, animations, or video in the opening, resist the temptation to talk over it. Remember, your customer is focused on your laptop screen. Then, if your presentation has a main menu, briefly explain the "pathways" or segments so your customer understands the design, format, and intention of your presentation.

SST-10—Take the Lead Initially

During your presentation, it's important to take the lead at first and pick which path your customer will see. You want to stay in control at the beginning for two reasons: First, you know what's in your presentation and how to find it; and second, you have learned what information he or she wants to see because you have already established rapport and begun to qualify the customer.

SST-11—Avoid Reading the Screen

Always add to your presentation in your own words (Figure 2-2). Don't simply read each bullet point on the screen. You will only insult your customer's intelligence.

Figure 2-2. Add to the presentation in your own words.

Relax. Your customer will be reading the screen all by himself or herself. Assume this will happen, encourage your customer to have fun with it, and focus your efforts on explaining how the information applies to your customer's situation or provides a solution to his or her needs and concerns.

SST-12—Talk to Your Customer, Not to Your Laptop

Don't make the mistake many novices do by talking only to your laptop screen. Occasionally pull back from your laptop, swivel your body toward the customer, look him or her straight in the eye, and talk about a key point. It's amazing how the customer will mirror your actions. Also, your customer will appreciate the chance to talk with you while you're in the middle of your presentation. Furthermore, every time you reestablish eye contact during the sales presentation, you have another opportunity to qualify the customer and receive feedback, too.

SST-13—Keep the Customer Involved

It's critical to keep your customer involved in your presentation. Here are a few good ideas on how you can do this:

- First, keep qualifying throughout your presentation. Find natural breaks to learn as much as you can about the company and its challenges.

- Next, ask for feedback on what the customer is seeing. Remember to use open-ended questions that start with *who, what, when, where,* and *how* to help stimulate discussions.

- Ask what the customer wants to see next. In this case, don't ask an open-ended question like, "What would you like to see next?" Instead, give the customer two or three options to choose from. This way, you're learning what your customer is interested in and you're refocusing his or her attention on your presentation.

- Let the customer "drive" by taking control of the mouse, trackpad or pointing device. Give him or her a chance to explore solo! This is the ultimate in keeping your customer involved in your sales material!

SST-14—Point with Your Finger Rather Than the Cursor

Use your finger or a pen to point at the screen rather than using the cursor. It's faster and easier than relying on the cursor to point the way. Plus it's much easier for your customer to see your finger than the tiny cursor on screen.

SST-15—Use *Minimize* to Jump between Presentations

Use the **Minimize** function within Windows 95 to jump from one basic presentation to another.

Let's say you're presenting product information and you want to compare prices between two different models. You have already created a separate worksheet in PowerPoint that shows these cost comparisons. From your main PowerPoint presentation, press the **Escape** key to quit **Slide Show View**. Then click

Cost Comparison

LaserPower 1000		TypeMaster 600
$ 3199	Base Price	$ 4199
199	Extra Paper Tray	–
99	Installation	129
89	Service Contract	119
$ 3586	Total Cost	$ 4566
$ 977	Savings	

Figure 2-3. **Slide Show View** in PowerPoint displays the content full screen with no toolbars showing.

the **Minimize** button to reduce the presentation to the **Taskbar**. Your show will still be active.

Next open your premade cost-comparison worksheet from a **Shortcut** you have previously made on your **Desktop** screen. The worksheet will open in **Slide View**, the "working" view. Click on **Slide Show View** to pop the worksheet full screen and review the information with your customer (Figure 2-3).

When you're done, press **Escape**, minimize the worksheet, click on your first presentation on the **Taskbar**, and then click on **Slide Show View**, and you're right back where you left off.

SST-16—Pay Attention to Body Language

Always pay attention to the customer's body language. If he or she is interested and excited, continue. But if the customer is looking at a watch or not paying attention, immediately stop, close your laptop, and change direction. Say something like, "With the time we have left, what are the most important issues you would like to discuss?" Then wait for a response. If the customer is noncommittal, take the lead and identify two or three topics you want to discuss; then press on.

Summary

This chapter has reviewed the first 16 of 30 *shoulder-to-shoulder* techniques. After you have tried some of these techniques, you'll see that they are easy to do. Soon you'll begin to discover ways to use your own style to make the presentation even more fun.

How to Avoid the Pitfalls in Presenting with Your Laptop

Pitfall	*Try This*
I'm usually in a hurry and sometimes forget to boot up and hit **Suspend** before the call.	• Put a reminder note on your car dashboard or on the outside of your laptop case where you will see it. • Rely on the reminder note until you establish the habit of booting up your laptop, launching your show, finding the right screen, and setting the system to **Suspend** before the call begins. You can even do this in an elevator. It just takes a moment.
Sometimes I use my laptop too soon during the call.	• Remember that a laptop is simply another sales tool, and a sales call with a laptop is still the same kind of call you have always made. • Review your basic sales process. First, establish rapport with the customer, and second, begin the qualification process before reaching for the laptop. • Practice transitional phrases that work well for you. Memorize several of them. That will help you remember to wait until the right moment to transition to the use of your laptop. • Let the customer guide your use of the laptop. When you hear a question or concern for which you can show an answer or suggest a solution, use a transitional phrase to move to the laptop at that point in the conversation.
I can't seem to get *"shoulder-to-shoulder"* with my customers. Most of them don't want to move from behind the desk.	• Look for a neutral selling spot such as a coffee table with a sofa or chairs. • When a natural transition point presents itself, stand up, move to the neutral location, and say something like, "Come on and let me show you something interesting that I believe will answer your question." When you move, the customer is likely to move with you. • When no neutral location is available, open your laptop, face it toward your customer, and then walk around to the other side of the desk. Kneel down by the customer at eye level and proceed.

How to Avoid the Pitfalls in Presenting with Your Laptop (*Cont.*)

Pitfall	Try This
Customers in my industry often have no table or surface on which I can to set my laptop.	• It's OK to sit *shoulder-to-shoulder* and use the laptop on your knees if you have no other alternative. • If the lack of a surface is the norm for your sales calls, invest in a small portable table or stand, and bring it with you. Several collapsible varieties are available.
Sometimes my customers become too focused on the laptop.	• Remain in control of your sales call at all times. • Push your chair back from the table and shift or swivel your body to face the customer directly. • Close the lid of your laptop. • Look at the customer's eyes and ask a direct question or two until he or she refocuses on you.
What if the customer wants to see things I don't want him to see in my presentation?	• If possible, preplan the development of your presentation so that every part of it is "fair game" and can be seen by prospects and customers. • Take the lead in choosing which information to see. • If the customer asks about information you would rather not show, explain it verbally in general terms and then click to new information.
I need to show four different presentations during a single sales call. How can I keep from getting mixed up?	• Create **Shortcuts** on your **Desktop** screen for every presentation you need to use. • Practice using **Minimize/Maximize** to move between PowerPoint presentations. • For moving between multimedia presentations, find the quickest way to exit the show you're in (often it's the **Escape** button on your keyboard), and then double-click on the next presentation **Shortcut**.

Practical Exercises

Exercise 2-1. Practice using **Suspend** and waking up your computer. Try suspending your laptop with a PowerPoint presentation already open.

Exercise 2-2. Brainstorm options for when you want to use a laptop on a sales call. For calls on new prospects, what information or qualifying questions do you want to ask before you transition to using your laptop? Think about different sales scenarios (in your business) and identify when you want to use your laptop with customers.

Exercise 2-3. Find natural breaks within your presentation to keep the customer involved. Open your presentation and look for natural opportunities to ask qualifying questions of your customer.

Exercise 2-4. Practice using the **Minimize** function as you jump from one presentation to another. Try using the techniques in SST-15. Choose two documents or presentations on your hard drive and practice jumping back and forth between them.

• CHAPTER 3 •

Ending the Call

Now that you've impressed the customer with your laptop and your verbal presentation, it's time to take the next steps to advance the sales process. Consider these *shoulder-to-shoulder* techniques.

SST-17—When Your Sales Call Is Complete, Choose *Suspend* and Close the Lid

When you're finished with your presentation, put your laptop computer to **Sleep** or **Suspend** and close the lid. The main benefit is to conserve battery power. Also, it's easy to wake the system back up if you need to make a presentation to someone else at the customer's location.

SST-18—Identify Next Steps

You'll want to answer any remaining questions and then identify what next steps to take as you move forward in the sales process. This could include meeting with others, scheduling a demonstration, testing your products at your customer's location, or using your laptop to deliver a proposal.

Whatever the next step, make sure you log it on your day-timer or contact management scheduling program and, most importantly, on the customer's calendar. Also, remember to ask for referrals regarding others you could go see.

SST-19—Be Prepared to Meet with and Present to Others

Many times your customer will want to show your presentation to others in the organization. The best approach is to make a group presentation on the spot. If you can't do it that day, how-

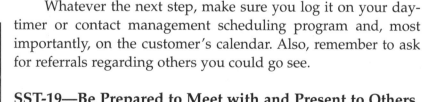

49

ever, be sure to ask to look at the conference room so you'll know what to expect when you use a projection system for a group presentation at your next appointment.

SST-20—Provide "Leave-Behinds"

Another key step in closing your call is to leave a brochure or follow-up information your customer can reference later. In addition, some salespeople carry one of the new ultra-small portable printers so they can print out key content screens for leave-behinds.

One suggestion, though. Make your printout *after* you have completed the call (but while you're still at the customer's location). That way, your customer won't have to wait while you connect the cords and print the document.

Also, many companies design laptop presentations for a dual purpose: to show during a sales call and to use as a giveaway so customers can load and explore the presentation at their leisure. If your customers request it, you can load your presentation onto their office computers while you're at their location. That way your presentation can act as a "silent salesperson" long after the sales call is over.

SST-21—Ask for a Business Card

Before you walk out the door, remember to ask for a business card and an e-mail address or fax number for your follow-up communication. With that information, you'll be sure to spell your customer's name and address correctly for your contact management software program. This also sets the stage for sending your thank-you letter.

Note: In Chapter 10 you'll find several sample templates you can use for sending thank-you letters.

SST-22—Send a Follow-Up Letter the Same Day

Try creating a lasting impression by faxing or e-mailing your thank-you letter that same day, directly from your laptop. You can send a fax from your home office, from a hotel room, or even from your car by hooking your cell phone directly into your laptop.

Stop by a computer retailer or cell phone equipment dealer for a demonstration on how easy it is to fax via your cell phone. Also, see Chapter 9 for more information about faxing from your laptop.

How to Avoid the Pitfalls in Ending the Call	
Pitfall	*Try This*
I shut down my laptop as the call ended, but my customer had additional questions.	• **Suspend** your laptop rather than shutting down at the end of your sales call. • It's much faster to "wake up" your computer than to boot up from scratch.
My customer was impatient as I hooked up my portable printer to print a document she needed.	• Save your printing process for after the call itself but while you're still at the customer's location. • Hook up your printer in the waiting area, a conference room, or another out-of-the-way spot so you can take you own time rather than your customer's.
If my customer wants a copy of my sales presentation, what problems could I run into if I try to load it onto his computer?	• Keep a copy of the necessary system parameters for your sales presentation with you. • Check with the customer to see if his/her system meets those minimum requirements for installation. If so, installation should proceed smoothly. • If the customer's equipment is on a radically different platform than yours (Mac versus PC, for example), say you'll need to check with your tech support people to see if the correct version is available. • If you're comfortable with the loading/installation procedure, go ahead and try it on your customer's system. • If you're not comfortable, simply leave a diskette or CD-ROM for the customer to install.
I left the call without identifying next steps.	• Go into every sales call with next steps already in mind. Know what you want and go for it! • Make it a personal rule never to leave a sales call without establishing appropriate next steps. • Create and send a "next-step" letter immediately after your call.

Summary

As you can see, the steps to ending your *shoulder-to-shoulder* call are quite similar to what you already do now. *The key is to advance your sales process to the next step.* And selling with your laptop is simple. It just takes a little practice to build your confidence in using a new sales tool. (Remember, you didn't learn how to sell in just one day, either.)

In many ways, using your laptop is just like faxing, using cell phones, and sending e-mail. After you've done it a few times, you'll wonder how you ever got along without it!

Practical Exercises

Exercise 3-1. Think of your next sales call. Brainstorm the next steps you want to complete (or suggest) after you're done with your presentation. Make a list of the questions you would want to ask or actions you could recommend to help advance your sales process. Take the list with you to your next call.

Exercise 3-2. Practice using the follow-up letter templates included in Chapter 10. Or create your own set of thank-you letter templates using the word processing software on your laptop. Write a thank-you letter and save it under an easy-to-remember filename. Each time you need to use the letter, open it, type in the new customer address and salutation, and then do a **Save As** to a different filename (usually the customer's last name). Use the new filename version to revise text and print the letter. That way your original follow-up letter is preserved in "template" form ready to go for the next new customer.

Exercise 3-3. Practice faxing or e-mailing a follow-up letter to someone you know. E-mail or fax directly from your laptop. Consult your user manual for setup instructions. Each manufacturer has a slightly different setup procedure. Get comfortable with the process so you can do it quickly and easily. Refer to the steps in Chapter 9 for more detailed information.

• CHAPTER 4 •

More Effective Group Presentations with Your Laptop

When you're presenting in front of a group, many of the *shoulder-to-shoulder* techniques you have just learned will still apply. In this chapter you'll discover a few others to help you become even more effective in delivering excellent group presentations. In addition, you'll also learn about some of the accessories you may need to make your group presentations easier and more comfortable.

Note: See Chapter 8 for more specific information on how to connect to projection systems, LCD panels, and TVs.

SST-23—Customize Your Presentation for the Customer

Launch your presentation before any of the attendees arrive. That way if you're using a basic PowerPoint presentation, you can put the show in **Slide Show View** with the customized first screen already prominently displayed—and everyone will be impressed as they first walk in the room (Figure 4-1).

SST-24—Focus Attention on You, Not on Your Presentation

It's important for you to remain the primary focus of the meeting. Remember, your presentation is there just to support you—not replace you.

SST-25—Begin without Your Laptop

Begin your presentation by standing away from your computer and the projection screen. Welcome the group, review your objec-

Figure 4-1. Show the customized first screen of your presentation in **Slide Show View** full screen with no toolbars showing.

tives, and distribute your agenda sheets and any other handouts. Verbally tee up what the group is about to see. It's also a good idea to make eye contact with each person for 5 to 10 seconds at a time as you conduct your welcome and review.

SST-26—Dim the Lights

When you're ready to use your laptop, dim the lights. This will focus the group's attention on the projection screen and help to build excitement and anticipation with your audience. You would be surprised how many salespeople fail to take this com- monsense step when they're in a group situation.

SST-27—Stay Fluid and Active throughout Presentation

As you proceed through your presentation, stay fluid and active, rather than static or glued to the same spot in the room. Move around. Try walking over to the screen and pointing to a key visual or bullet point. Occasionally walk to the side of the room and reestablish eye contact as you make a particular point.

SST-28—Keep the Group Involved

Encourage the group to stay involved. Even though there's a risk in asking the group for questions or feedback, the rewards far outweigh the alternatives: lack of interest, or worse yet, the dreaded "sleeping attendees syndrome"!

Try using the **Standby** button (or **Blank** button) on the projection system. This will cause the screen to go blank, giving you an opportunity to stop and ask questions at key points during the meeting. You'll keep the members of the group alert, renew their attention span, and refocus their eyes on you.

SST-29—Apply *Shoulder-to-Shoulder Selling* Techniques to Groups

Remember to use the same *shoulder-to-shoulder* techniques that apply to one-on-one sales presentations:

- In your own words, add to the content on each screen rather than reading each bullet point.

- Answer questions from the group by using the menus in advanced presentations to navigate to different content screens.

- Use the **Minimize** function to quickly jump back and forth between different basic presentations.

- Avoid talking over any audio or video segments so the group's attention can remain focused on the multimedia aspects of your show.

SST-30—Closing Tips

As you close your meeting, gain agreement on your next steps, ask for business cards, and send a follow-up letter as soon as possible to give all the attendees a lasting impression about your prompt professionalism.

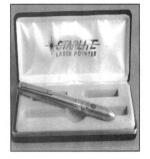

Accessories

Many projectors will have a remote control or remote mouse included with them. These are great for enhancing your freedom and delivery style, especially if you do a lot of group presentations.

A *remote mouse* is basically a remote control that allows you to walk, talk, and control your laptop while standing away from it. Most remote mouse systems require you to install a small piece of software on your laptop that will make the mouse compatible with your laptop's commands. This software is typically included in the package and comes with installation instructions.

Tip: Your remote mouse takes standard batteries, usually two AAA batteries. If you haven't used your remote mouse lately, be sure to check the batteries or replace them with new ones before you begin your next group presentation!

Laser pointers can be used to direct the group's attention to key areas on the projection screen. They are fun and easy to use and liven up your presentation.

Tip: If you choose to use a laser pointer, use it sparingly and keep your hand movements slow and deliberate. A little laser pointing goes a long way, and can be distracting to your audience if overused.

Summary

We hope you're now more comfortable with how and when to use your laptop in group situations and *shoulder-to-shoulder* with customers. As with anything new, practicing these techniques is critical to raising your confidence level and increasing your sales effectiveness.

How to Avoid the Pitfalls in Making Group Presentations

Pitfall	Try This
I usually start right in showing my slides.	• Keep the room lights up as the group assembles. • If you're showing a basic presentation, customize the first screen and display it on the projection screen. • Before you start to show slides, keep the lights up as you welcome the group, review your objectives, and tee up your presentation. • Hand out agenda sheets and collateral material before dimming the lights. • Build excitement as you introduce yourself and your presentation and then begin.
I don't have a remote mouse, so I tend to stay pretty close to my laptop as I present.	• Get comfortable with the position of **Page Up/Page Down** buttons on your laptop keyboard (or use the up/down arrows) so you can find them easily in a darkened room. • Deliberately move away from your laptop after every few slides. Walk to the other side of the room. • Step to the projection screen and use your finger or pointing device to draw attention to several key points. • Then move back to the laptop and click to the next slide.
I notice people start falling asleep or drifting off when I'm only halfway through my presentation.	• Provide natural breaks every 10 minutes where you turn up the room lights, place the projection system on **Standby**, and ask a question or two of your audience. • If there is no **Standby** or **Pause** button on the projector, place the lens cap over the lens to block out the light. Turn up the room lights and review two or three key points from the last few slides.
I like to ask for feedback, but sometimes the group gets away from me.	• It's your presentation, so it's up to you to keep attention focused on you. • Use the lens cover or **Standby** button to pause the screen image. Stop and summarize the comments you have heard. • Suggest any nonrelated topics be tabled for another time. Create a "bucket" list for a later discussion. • Dim the lights and return to your slide presentation.

Practical Exercises

Exercise 4-1. Find a quiet room where you will not be disturbed. Hook your laptop to a projector, LCD panel, or TV (see instructions in Chapter 8) and practice delivering your presentation by yourself aloud two or three times, or until you feel comfortable. You may discover that you would like to add information, key points, or even artwork. You can easily change a basic presentation to add or subtract more information. With an advanced presentation (not so easy to change), write down other "talking points" that occur to you and keep them in your laptop carrying case. They'll be handy when you deliver your next presentation.

Exercise 4-2. When you're ready, gather a friendly audience and practice delivering your presentation in front of people who will give you positive, constructive criticism.

Exercise 4-3. Write down questions regarding your sales presentation that will encourage feedback from the group. Make note of the exact points in the show when you would ask these questions. Better yet, create new slides in your basic presentation that will display these questions and give you natural opportunities to stop and refocus the group's attention on you.

• Part 2 •

Creating Powerful Presentations

• CHAPTER 5 •

How to Create Your Own PowerPoint Presentation in 30 Minutes

Now that you have learned some simple techniques for preparing your presentation, delivering it in a sales call, and ending your call effectively, you're ready to take the next step and create a basic presentation of your own. With the excellent presentation software on the market today, you can create a useful working presentation in 30 minutes or less. This chapter will get you started; and Chapter 6, "Suggestions for Making Your Presentation Look Great," will give you some easy tips that will help you refine your presentation to look interesting and professional.

About the Software

When you're building your own basic presentation, start with an easy software package like Microsoft PowerPoint or Adobe Persuasion. If your PC laptop has a Windows 95 or newer operating system, it's likely that the Microsoft Office suite of software products is already loaded onto your system. PowerPoint is one of those options.

For the purposes of this chapter and the next, we'll refer to Microsoft PowerPoint because it's the presentation software you probably have on your laptop computer. If your system does not have PowerPoint or presentation software of some kind, contact your computer store.

Believe it or not, the best way to become familiar with the functions and features of any new software is to read the user's guide. If tackling the entire manual at once seems too daunting, just read the introduction, the setup instructions, and the first

61

chapter. Then launch the program and begin to experiment. Refer to the user's guide as needed.

In the case of PowerPoint, the user's guide is well written and easy to follow. Plus all of the information from the user's guide—and more—is available at the touch of a button when you're using the program. Just click on the **Help** icon found on the standard toolbar (Figure 5-1).

If you're buying PowerPoint, it's best to get the latest version, unless most of your colleagues are using an older version. In that case, buy what they're using. It will be easier for you to share files. Another strategy is to encourage the company to upgrade across the board to the highest available version.

A Little Organization First

Before you begin to create a new presentation, take a little time to organize your thoughts and materials. And whether you're

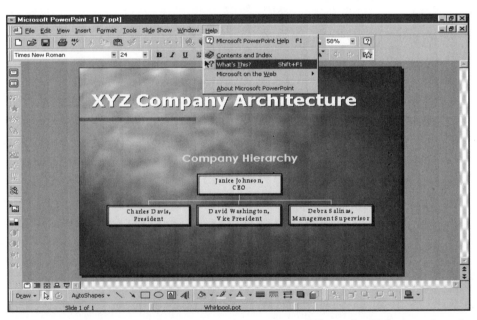

Figure 5-1. If you need help working in PowerPoint, just click on the **Help** icon found on the standard toolbar.

building your own presentation or providing input to a development team who will build one for you, the key to creating a powerful presentation is to start with the audience in mind.

What type of prospects and customers will view your presentation? Are they decision makers, influencers, or end users? What information will your customers or prospects want to see? What questions will they ask? What are your best answers? What solutions or remedies can you offer to typical customer problems? What information is most important to show first? To show second? To show third? These are all excellent questions to consider. They'll help you get started organizing the material you need for your presentation.

We suggest that you design your presentation with the typical customer or prospect in mind. Also keep in mind the overall purpose and goals for your sales call. Before you write anything down, think about what specific actions you want your customers to take. Then gather your materials, organize them, and write your content logically by topic in the same way you would deliver a successful presentation. Drive the organization of the presentation toward aiding your customer to take the desired action.

Here are a few possible ways to organize your content:

Suggested Structure 1	Suggested Structure 2	Suggested Structure 3
1. Opening	1. Overview	1. Company History and Corporate Organization
2. About Your Company	2. Product Features, Advantages, and Benefits	2. Why Choose Your Company?
3. Overview of Your Products/Services	3. Product Categories	3. Products/Services
4. Competitive Advantages and Benefits	4. Applications	4. Compare & Contrast with Competition
5. Common Questions and Answers	5. Data Sheets, Tech Specs, and Test Results	5. Case Studies and Testimonials
6. Next Steps/Actions	6. Pricing	6. Ordering Information
7. Closing	7. Availability/Shipping	7. Contact Information

There is nothing magic about the number seven. Your presentation may have four topic headings or fifteen. We offer these seven suggestions simply because they represent the common organizational structure of many sales presentations we have created for many companies.

In the long run, you may want to follow the structure of the sales presentation you already have, provided it works well for you. But if you're creating a new presentation, the point is to think about all the products, services, and benefits your company has to offer. Organize this content into ways that can be easily viewed and quickly understood by your customers.

Built-in Options for Different "Looks"

You have thought about your sales presentation, you've organized your materials, and you're ready to go, but you don't know where to start. Relax. You don't have to be a good writer or graphic designer to create a good-looking, persuasive presentation. You can use one of the templates offered in PowerPoint. The software comes with two main template types: content templates and design templates.

Design templates offer you more than a dozen "looks," color schemes, and options that have been designed by graphic artists. These templates help you create a professional, custom look for your presentation. You can also modify the templates to your needs.

Content templates are premade types of presentations with suggested content outlines already organized to help you insert your own information in a logical way. They also contain design formats and color schemes to help you with the graphical look of your slides. Content templates give you a choice of more than 20 presentation types, such as "Project Overview," "Business Plan," "Recommending a Strategy," and "Selling Your Ideas," for example.

Start your presentation by launching PowerPoint (from the **Start** button on the **Taskbar**, point to **Programs** and click on **Microsoft PowerPoint**). The system will show you a dialog box that lets you start a new presentation in three ways:

1. Choose the **AutoContent** wizard.

2. Choose a design template.

3. Start with a blank presentation.

Creating a New Presentation Using *AutoContent* Wizard

When you select the **AutoContent** wizard to start your presentation, you can choose from more than 20 presentation types (Figure 5-2). You're directed to choose how the show will be used (as a formal presentation, for informal meetings, handouts, etc).

Next, you can choose a presentation style (whether you want an on-screen presentation, overhead transparencies, 35mm slides, or printed handouts). Then, you'll be asked to enter information that will appear on your opening screen.

Once your choices are made, click **Finish**, and you'll see an outline that suggests possible content. You'll also see a small sample of the design template the system has chosen for you.

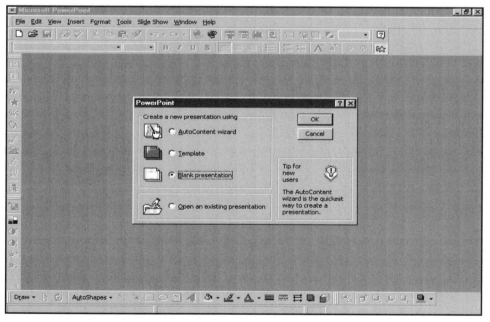

Figure 5-2. The **AutoContent** wizard in PowerPoint allows you to access predeveloped presentation content and graphic designs.

Now you can write your presentation in outline form, save it, and view it in **Slide View**. Save your presentation by finding the **File** menu and clicking **Save**; or use the keyboard command [Ctrl] + [S].

Creating a New Presentation Using a Design Template

When you launch PowerPoint and select the **Template** button from the dialog box, another dialog window appears with more than a dozen designs to choose from. As you click on each file, a preview appears.

When you select the design template you want, you'll see the **AutoLayout** dialog box. You're given a choice of two dozen different automatic slide layouts. Start with the **Title Slide**. The system takes you to **Slide View** (the main working view) and shows you where to type in a title and subtitle for your presentation.

Tip: Use the **Title Slide** to customize your presentation (Figure 5-3).

Wendover Foods

A Presentation for

Mr. Brent Jones

XYZ International, Ltd.

Figure 5-3. An example of a **Title Slide** you can use to customize a basic presentation.

Create new slides by going to the **Insert** menu and clicking **New Slide**. You can also get a new slide in two other ways: Click the **New Slide** icon on the standard toolbar, or use the keyboard command **[Ctrl] + [M]**.

Each time you call for a new slide, the **AutoLayout** dialog box appears. You must choose the slide layout you want.

The system shows you where to add text on every new slide. A message like "Click to add title" and "Click to add text" or "Double-click to add org chart" will appear. You'll see that you can create text and some artwork right on your slide without using any other programs. (See Chapter 6 for details about adding artwork in programs other than PowerPoint.)

Save your presentation—from the **File** menu, click **Save**; or use the keyboard command **[Ctrl] + [S]**.

Starting with a Blank Presentation

Launch PowerPoint and select **Blank Presentation** from the dialog box. The **AutoLayouts** will appear. Choose the **Title Slide** first, and then create new slides as you wish.

The background will be blank until you choose to create one. The slide layouts, color schemes, backgrounds, and design templates can be accessed from the **Format** menu at any time.

As with any new presentation, you can write text in **Slide View** or **Outline View**. Also, you can move slides around easily in **Slide Sorter View** or see the presentation full screen in **Slide Show View** (hit the **Escape** key to return to **Slide View**).

Use the **Slide Master View** to apply artwork or text to all the slides in your show. These views are all accessed from the **View** menu or from the icons on your working screen, bottom left corner.

Save your presentation—from the **File** menu, click **Save**; or use the keyboard command **[Ctrl] + [S]**.

Summary

In this chapter, we started by getting organized and learning three simple ways to create a new presentation using PowerPoint

How to Avoid the Pitfalls in Creating Your Own Presentation

Pitfall	*Try This*
I have too much material to fit into one presentation.	• If you had only 5 minutes to complete a sales call, what would you absolutely have to show your prospect? Start with those materials and talking points. • What would you show if you had 10 minutes for a presentation? Add those items. • What would you show if your sales call were 20 minutes long? 30 minutes?
I'm having trouble getting started.	• Try creating a new presentation using the **AutoContent** wizard. • Select the type of presentation you want, and follow the prompts about what kind of text to write. • Look at the content in different types of presentations from the **AutoContent** wizard. See which one works well for you. • Choose one. Then modify the presentation to fit your needs.
I've created five new slides, but I want to put a new one between slides 3 and 4.	• Go to **Slide Sorter View**. The slides will be small. • Move your cursor between slides 3 and 4. • Select **New Slide** (from **Insert** menu or keyboard command **[Ctrl] + [M]**). • Double-click on the new slide to return to **Slide View** to add new content.
It seems like a lot of work to write my company name on every slide.	• Write it in once on the **Slide Master**. • Go to the **View** menu and click **Master**. • Write your text. Size it. Click and drag the text box to the position you want. • Return to **Slide View**. Your company name will appear in the same spot on all your slides.
When I look at my presentation full screen (**Slide Show View**), I don't know how to get out of this view.	• Hit the **Escape** button on your keyboard (upper left corner).

software. With the exercises at the end of this chapter, you'll see that it only takes about 30 minutes to create a new presentation you can use right away. In the next chapter, you'll find out how to work with your new presentation to give it pace and visual interest.

Practical Exercises

Exercise 5-1. Create a new presentation using the **AutoContent** wizard. Select the type of presentation you want. Use **Outline View** to write two or three slides. Switch to **Slide View** to see how your presentation looks.

Exercise 5-2. Create a new presentation using the design template feature. Preview several designs and choose one. Fill in text for the **Title Slide** and two or three additional slides of your choosing.

Exercise 5-3. Create a new presentation using the blank presentation feature. Write two slides in **Slide View**. Then select **Outline View** and write two additional slides. Practice switching between **Slide View, Outline View, Slide Sorter View,** and **Slide Show View**. What can you do in each view?

Exercise 5-4. If you have an existing sales presentation, practice delivering it out loud. Time yourself. Modify your show to be longer or shorter, depending on your needs.

Suggestions for Making Your Presentation Look Great

How to Get Started

If you're creating a basic presentation from scratch and you have not read Chapter 5, go back and read it now. It will help you to organize your content and set it up in PowerPoint. In about 30 minutes, you'll have a head start on creating a good basic presentation.

In this chapter, we're assuming that you have already made a basic presentation or that you're comfortable with PowerPoint or some other presentation software program. Now you'd like to create a new, high-impact presentation. You're ready to refine your presentation to become as attractive and powerful as possible.

One of the best ways to get started making your presentation look great is to think of its impact on your customers in terms of two separate ideas:

1. *Content.* The words and any informative tables and charts
2. *Design.* The look and feel of the presentation, including overall design, choice of artwork, colors, backgrounds, photos, and typefaces for headlines and body text

Your goal for content is to make it simple, clear, and easy to see on screen. Your goal for design is to create a unified, consistent look for the presentation and enhance it with appropriate colors and graphics.

Tips for Improving the Impact of Your Presentations

You can make any presentation you create more visually interesting and verbally compelling to your customers. In this section you'll find several tips for writing content and choosing the right typeface, colors, and artwork that will dramatically improve the visual impact and clarity of your presentations.

Content

Once you've organized your content into main topic headings or categories, it's time to write (or rewrite) the "guts" of your presentation. By following these simple rules, you can write livelier, more interesting text that will capture the attention of your customers and more easily persuade them to your point of view.

Keep the Text Simple. Your customers and prospects don't need all the detail all at once. Focus on one key thought or idea per presentation screen. Use bullet points to illustrate that idea. Write in short phrases rather than in long sentences or paragraph-length blocks of text.

Use the "Active" Voice. As you craft each phrase, learn to use the *active* rather than *passive* voice. *Voice* refers to which form of the verb you choose. Learn to distinguish between active and passive voice.

- *Active* voice means that the subject of the sentence *acts*. As a result, the phrase becomes stronger, more powerful, more direct, and more visual.
- *Passive* voice means the subject of the sentence is *acted upon*. The phrase becomes weaker, less direct, more awkward, and harder for the reader to visualize.

Compare these examples:

The Midwest territory *was canvassed* by the district manager. (*passive voice*)

The district manager *canvassed* the Midwest territory. (*active voice*)

In 1999, the industry *was led* in product quality by Acme Sportswear. (*passive voice*)

In 1999, Acme Sportswear *led* the industry in product quality. (*active voice*)

The new drug *is now being prescribed* by Ohio veterinarians. (*passive voice*)

Ohio veterinarians now *prescribe* the new drug. (*active voice*)

A 25 percent jump *was experienced* by sales in the Pacific Rim. (*passive voice*)

Pacific Rim sales *experienced* a 25 percent jump last quarter. (*active voice*)

Write a Simple, High-Impact Headline for Every Screen. For example:

Acme Sportswear Takes Top Spot

Homebuyers Choose Quest Flooring First

Protective Outerwear Now in 15 Styles

Our Products Feature Unmatched Benefits

Use Headlines with Active, Present-Tense Verbs. For example:

LaserPower 100 *Sustains* Performance

Ace Marine *Wins* Quality Award

WestBank *Offers* the Lowest Interest Rate

At Bradley Foods, We *Deliver* What We *Promise*

Figures 6-1 and 6-2 compare the use of active versus passive voice in headlines and body copy.

Emphasize Key Points. Use text and graphics to draw the eye to the main point on each screen—especially with tables and charts. Make the important numbers red or some other color that stands out from the rest. You can also use circles and arrows for dramatic emphasis (Figure 6-3).

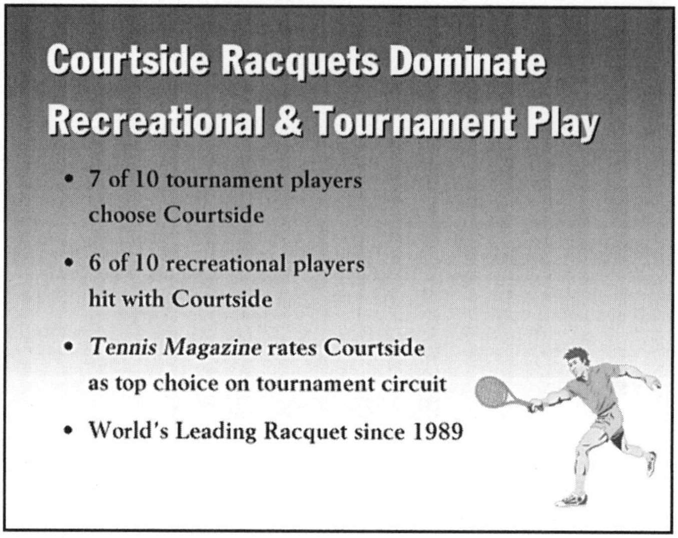

Courtside Racquets Dominate Recreational & Tournament Play

- 7 of 10 tournament players choose Courtside
- 6 of 10 recreational players hit with Courtside
- *Tennis Magazine* rates Courtside as top choice on tournament circuit
- World's Leading Racquet since 1989

Figure 6-1. Use this! Write shorter headlines in active voice. Use short, punchy bullets with present-tense verbs. In slides, use numerals.

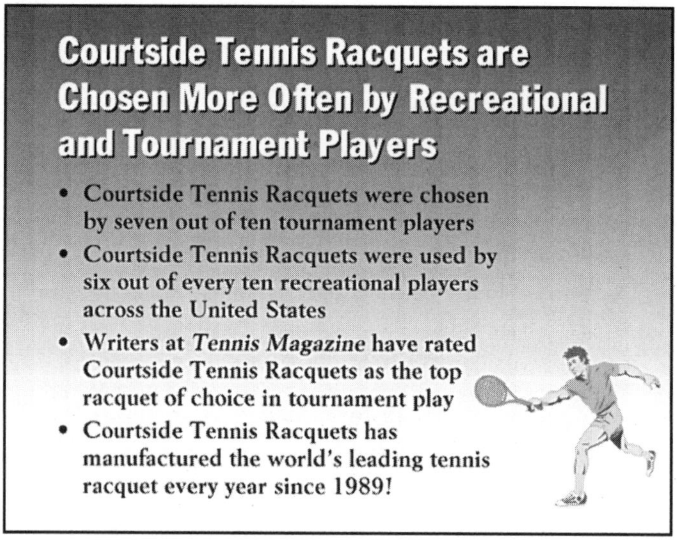

Courtside Tennis Racquets are Chosen More Often by Recreational and Tournament Players

- Courtside Tennis Racquets were chosen by seven out of ten tournament players
- Courtside Tennis Racquets were used by six out of every ten recreational players across the United States
- Writers at *Tennis Magazine* have rated Courtside Tennis Racquets as the top racquet of choice in tournament play
- Courtside Tennis Racquets has manufactured the world's leading tennis racquet every year since 1989!

Figure 6-2. Not this! Avoid long headlines in passive voice. Avoid long blocks of text in full-sentence form. Avoid spelling out numerals.

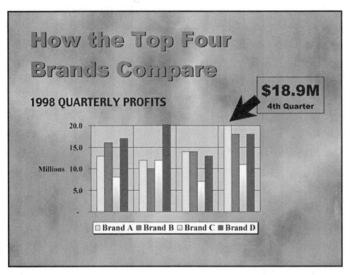

Figure 6-3. Draw the eye toward key points with a highlight color, or even an arrow or circle for special emphasis.

Create a Summary Screen Every Few Screens as a Review Opportunity. The use of a review screen is up to you. Some salespeople like them and think they work well, while others don't. Your software is highly flexible, so you can do what's best for you.

Intersperse Key Qualifying Questions throughout Your Presentation. Design the questions to prompt customer feedback, to stimulate comments and interaction, and to move your sales process forward. By using a separate screen or slide for each question, you'll help to break up the flow of the presentation. Also, you'll have natural opportunities to reestablish eye contact with your customer as you ask the qualifying question and solicit feedback (Figures 6-4 and 6-5).

Use Effective Testimonials or "Outquotes" from Key People Whom Your Customers Will Recognize. A well-placed outquote

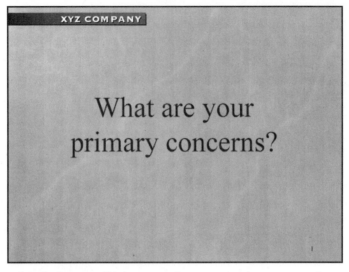

Figure 6-4. Example of a key qualifying question you can intersperse throughout your presentation to encourage feedback.

Figure 6-5. A key qualifying question like this gives you a natural chance to pause and reestablish eye contact with your customer.

"Technology has expanded markets exponentially and, in turn, forced salespeople to shift their approach to these markets. It's basically a whole new ballgame out there."

— MARGARET DANIELSON, XYZ INC.

Figure 6-6. Combine a large head-and-shoulders photo with a testimonial quote for high impact.

from the right person can have high impact on your audience. For the most powerful impact, combine the quotation on screen with a large head-and-shoulders photo of the person you're quoting (Figure 6-6).

Combine the Power of Sound with Text and a Photo. Newer versions of PowerPoint allow you to record sound right from your laptop using a built-in microphone. You can record testimonials from satisfied customers and combine a short "soundbite" with photos and text for tremendous impact. It's easy. Check your *PowerPoint User's Guide* and hardware manual.

Use Video—Even in PowerPoint. A video testimonial is even more powerful. With a video camera, the right connection cords, and your laptop, you can capture a video testimonial and insert it into your basic presentation. It's not as difficult as you might think. Check your *PowerPoint User's Guide* and hardware manual.

Look and Design

Take Advantage of "White" Space. Avoid crowding your screen with complicated visuals. Use the "white" (open) space already available. The screen doesn't need to be covered with text or graphics (Figures 6-7 and 6-8).

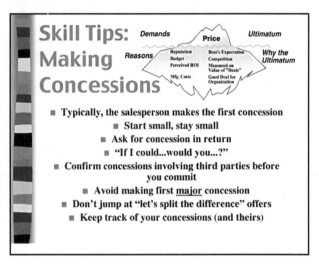

Figure 6-7. Example of a screen too crowded with text and graphics.

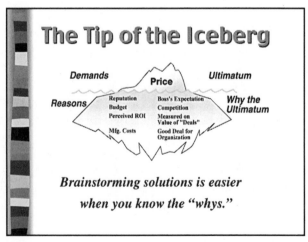

Figure 6-8. This screen shows a more pleasing combination of graphics, text, and white space.

Create Variety in Visuals. Avoid five bar charts in a row, for example. Mix it up.

Backgrounds Should Be Simple. They can have strong design elements, but should not obscure the text. Avoid backgrounds that dominate with a heavy color, busy design, or strong photos. Graphics and photos are fine, but when used as a background, they can fight with your text (Figure 6-9).

Create a "Master Page" to Establish a Consistent Look. Here you can designate a background design, logo, or other standard features you want to appear on every screen in your show (Figure 6-10).

Choose Appropriate Colors. Use color and design to complement—not detract from—your overall corporate image. Also, keep your audience in mind when choosing colors. Is your audience conservative? Upbeat? Cutting edge? Traditional? Corporate? Adjust colors accordingly.

Figure 6-9. Start with a simple background. Use high-contrast text.

Figure 6-10. The "master slide" in PowerPoint lets you select graphics and text that will appear on every slide in your presentation. You only have to place them once, but you can change them at any time by returning to the master slide.

Use Color on Your Screens, but Don't Overuse It. The color ought to emphasize and enhance your message, not overshadow it.

Use Artwork and Visuals as Needed. Logos, photos, graphs, charts, line drawings, and color illustrations are interesting and attract attention, but they can distract if overused. Ask yourself if each graphic element will complement or detract from the main thought on each content screen (Figure 6-11).

Make Sure Your Artwork Is Large Enough to Be Seen. If you're going to use a picture or graphic, choose a strong one and make it large enough for your customers to see from a distance of 2 or 3 feet. Also, don't crowd the graphic element by placing a lot of text on top of it (Figure 6-12).

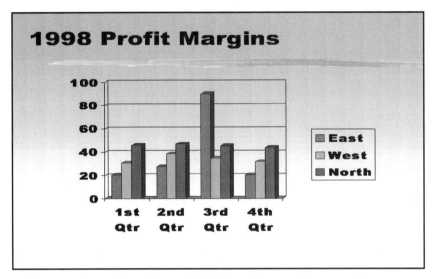

Figure 6-11. Charts and graphs enhance the look and persuasiveness of your presentation. They're easy to create, too.

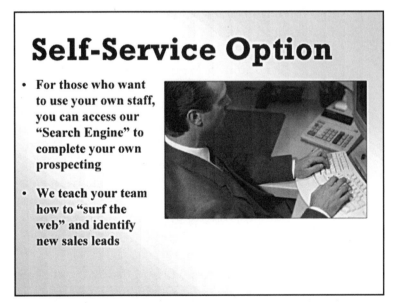

Figure 6-12. If you use photos or graphics, use them large enough to be easily seen.

It's a Good Idea to Use Transitions to Enhance the Look of Moving from One Screen to the Next, like a "Wipe Left" or "Checkerboard Down" or "Dissolve." From the **Slide Show** menu, choose **Slide Transition** and select the options you want. To view your transitions, you must go to full-screen **Slide Show View** (from **View** menu, choose **Slide Show**; when you're done, hit the **Escape** key to return to regular **Slide View**).

Use No More Than Three or Four Different Transition Types in a Single Show. A few of them go a long way. It's best not to use all the transitions the software offers. Be choosy.

Use the Same Transition When Moving from One Section to the Beginning of Another to Create Consistency and a Sense of Anticipation. For example, at the end of the first section, use a "fade." At the end of the second section, use a "fade" again, and so on.

Use Music or Sound Clips for the Opening, Closing, and Key Transition Phases of the Presentations. A standard set of sounds is already included on your system. From the PowerPoint slide on which you want sound, go to the **Insert** menu and choose **Movies and Sound**. Then click **Sound from Gallery** or **Sound from File** and follow the prompts.

These "built-in" sounds already on your laptop may not work for your particular show. If not, you can use sounds from CD-ROMs and diskettes. Many sound and music libraries are available on CD, tape, and diskette. Make sure to look for those that have already established the necessary permissions and clearances for you to use the clips.

Tip: From PowerPoint, click on the **Help** icon at any time for excellent directions on how to find a sound or music clip already on your laptop, or how to access other prerecorded sounds from other files or external CDs and diskettes.

You're the Designer: Making Your Own "Look"

If you have a marketing department that will make a basic presentation for you, fine. That saves you the work. On the other hand, it prevents you from having fun as you explore ways to make your own presentation look great.

If you have an opportunity to create your own presentation, you also have the chance to become the "designer" and establish just the right "look" and "feel" you desire. Here are a few rules of thumb about design that will help you start out on the right foot.

Let Yourself Be Creative. If you can imagine it, you can make it happen. Ask yourself what kind of presentation have you always wanted to have. What elements would you incorporate? What information is most powerful and persuasive to show during a sales call? If you could have that information in a different format, what format would you like? Tables? Charts? Graphs? Photos? Special colors? Animations? Testimonials? Sound? Video? Ask yourself, "Why not?" Then go for it!

Use Templates and Backgrounds Already Available in PowerPoint. These have been developed by professional graphic designers and adhere to the characteristics of good design that we have discussed in Chapter 5 and in this chapter.

> *Advantage.* It's the easiest way to make your presentation background look good.

> *Disadvantage.* Every company that uses PowerPoint has the same standard templates and backgrounds.

Or Establish Your Own Custom Design. Launch PowerPoint, choose **Blank Presentation**, and select the **Title Slide** from the **New Slide** dialog box.

- Now find the **Slide Master**. From the **View** menu, select **Master** and then click **Slide Master**.

- Another way to reach the **Slide Master** is to find the **Slide View** icon on your toolbar, then hold the **Shift** key down (on your keyboard), and click the **Slide View** icon. Either way, you'll reach **Slide Master** view.

Use this view to select a premade background or apply a background of your own. From the **Slide Master** you can insert logos, dates, times, footers, and slide numbers on all the slides in your show. Do it once on the **Slide Master**, and it's done for every slide in the show. When you're finished designing the **Slide Master**, hold the **Shift** key down and click the **Slide View** icon, which will return you to **Slide View**.

Find the Color Scheme You Like. You have a choice of several different professionally developed color schemes that coordinate well together. You can designate your own color choices for the background titles, body text, and graphics, too. Plus, you don't have to be on the **Slide Master** to change color schemes for the entire slide show. Simply go to the **Format** menu and choose **Slide Color Scheme** or **Background** to pick from several professionally designed color schemes or follow the prompts to create your own color combinations.

Match Your Company's Established Color Scheme as Closely as You Can. Needless to say, this applies only if your company has a set corporate color scheme. Unlike other full-function desktop publishing programs, PowerPoint does not allow you to designate process color the same way a print company does to print a full-color piece. As a result, it will be difficult for you to match any CMYK percentages (cyan, magenta, yellow, and black) or RGB percentages (red, green, and blue) exactly. You'll have to "eyeball" the color from your screen. If you're color blind, get a colleague to help you.

Use *Slide View* to Add Text. Click on the **New Slide** icon (or choose **New Slide** from the **Insert** menu) to create a new slide. Every time you choose **New Slide**, you are offered a number of premade layouts from which to choose. Twelve layouts at a time show in the dialog window. Be sure to use the slider at the right of the dialog window to view all the layout choices. Click on one of them to select.

Break a Long Show into Sections. If you have a large show, break it into sections; use different color backgrounds on each section.

Note: Each section must be its own file with its own separate **Slide Master**. To move back and forth between sections, open all sections. Each section will appear as a separate button on the **Taskbar**. You can click on the **Taskbar** to make any section active. You can also jump between sections by minimizing and maximizing (see the Appendix).

Know Your Corporate Parameters. Make use of your corporate materials—know the parameters. Maybe you have flexibility; maybe you don't. Use the correct logos, corporate artwork, type fonts, and type sizes.

Use the Graphics That Count. Ask your marketing department or corporate headquarters to provide you with electronic files of your company's official logo and any other official graphic elements.

Create Simple Charts to Illustrate a Point. You can create bar charts, organizational charts, and other simple graphics by clicking on the **New Slide** icon and choosing an **AutoLayout** with a bar chart, table, or organizational chart. When the new slide appears, double-click in the designated area to create the chart or table. The software is easy to follow and allows you to create the graphic right there. Once you have entered your information, the system adds the chart or table to your new slide.

Resist Using All the Bells and Whistles. Just because you can use all the features of PowerPoint or any other basic presentation software doesn't mean you should. As the world of computers puts the once highly specialized world of graphic design and word processing at our fingertips, some caution is in order. Resist the temptation to use 15 different typefaces in one show. Also, resist using a lot of clip art, unless that's the look and feel you want. You should avoid using every available color. You'll look like a rank amateur!

The ability to combine graphic elements tastefully and effectively is still the province of the professional graphic designer. By using the tips in this chapter, however, you can master a few simple techniques that will help to make your presentation look more professional.

Tips for Using Type

Test Content Screens for Readability As You Begin to Create Them. Can you read the text on your presentation from 2 or 3 feet away from the laptop screen? If you're unsure, ask a colleague to read your presentation and offer feedback.

Use Screens with Fewer Words and Larger Type. Use body type no smaller than 20 points; 24-point type is better.

Use Uppercase and Lowercase for Readability. Except perhaps for short headlines, avoid using all capital letters for text because they're too hard to read.

Stick with One Typeface or Font—or a Maximum of Two. This improves the professional look and makes your presentation simple and attractive to the eye. If you use two fonts, use one font for headlines and captions and the other for body text.

Combine a Serif Font with a Sans Serif Font If You're Using Two Fonts. Like the body text in this book, a *serif* font has little hooks or lines that extend from the ends and edges of each character. A *sans serif* font (meaning "without serifs") is straight and smooth without any extending hooks or lines. Serif is the traditional font style used for body text in newspapers and magazines. Sans serif is considered more modern.

- Times Roman, Palatino, Garamond, and Novarese are well-known examples of serif fonts:

Times Roman
Palatino
Garamond
Novarese

- Futura, Helvetica, and Arial are common sans serif fonts:

Futura
Helvetica
Arial

Use Strong Contrasts between Background and Text. In fact, contrasts are critical. Use either a dark background with lighter text or a light background with darker text.

Use Reversed Type Sparingly. Reversed type means the type is white or light against a dark or black background. It's effective as an accent, but can be hard to read, especially if the type is too small. Whatever color combination you choose for text and background, take an objective look at it. If your own eyes grow tired after a few screens, change the color scheme and strengthen the contrasts. Your goal is to make every screen *attractive* rather than *annoying* to your customers.

Use *WordArt* Styles Sparingly. A little goes a long way when you're using the **WordArt** feature in PowerPoint. This feature allows you to write text on your slide, select the text box, and then apply special characteristics to the words themselves by clicking on the **WordArt** icon. These effects are fun when applied to two or three words and when used only as an accent. Otherwise, they're hard to read, kitschy, and annoying if overused (Figure 6-13).

Choose Bright Headline Colors. Use colors like yellow or red. Or use white or silver gray against a dark background. The colors you choose depend on your background and overall design. Use colors that make sense, and within that general rule, choose bright contrasts for headlines.

Tips for Incorporating Artwork

In PowerPoint you can easily create tables, bar charts, and organizational charts. You can draw shapes or use the many available

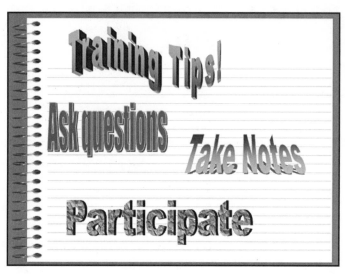

Figure 6-13. Special effects for type can be effective if they are used sparingly.

AutoShapes such as squares, circles, rectangles, arrows, stars, crosses, and ellipses. Also, it's easy to write text on any of these shapes. Most of these objects can be created and inserted right from the slide you're working on. Just choose the correct toolbar. Keep in mind that the best way to learn how to incorporate artwork into your presentation is by consulting your *PowerPoint User's Guide* or by using the detailed **Help** menus available within the software itself.

Please read the following section for a quick overview on creating and inserting different types of graphic elements, and then check your *PowerPoint User's Guide* for complete details.

Insert a table:

- Select **New Slide** and choose **Table** from the **AutoLayout** dialog box.

- When the new slide appears, double-click on the **Table** icon.

- PowerPoint offers a dialog box in which you can designate the number of rows and columns your table will have. Then the system launches a Microsoft Word table cell.

- Fill in the cells with text.

- You can edit the text, size it, and change fonts while in the Word table cell.

- When you're finished, click anywhere off the table, and PowerPoint will return you to the slide. You'll see the finished table.

Insert an organizational chart:

- Select **New Slide** and choose **Organization Chart** from the **AutoLayout** dialog box.

- When the new slide appears, double-click on the **Org Chart** icon.

- PowerPoint offers a **Microsoft Organization Chart** window in which you can follow simple directions to create the organizational chart. You can type in names, titles, and comments; add levels; and move boxes easily.

- When you're finished, close the window, click **Yes** when you're asked if you want to update the new object in **AutoShapes**, and your new organizational chart will appear on your slide.

- To edit it, double-click on the chart and you'll be returned to the working view (Figure 6-14).

Insert a bar chart:

- Select **New Slide** and choose any of the **AutoLayouts** that show a chart.

- When the new slide appears, double-click on the **Chart** icon. You will see an **AutoShapes Datasheet** window offering table cells you can use to add text and number values for your chart. You'll also see a picture of the chart itself. Every time you change a value, the corresponding bar will change on the chart itself.

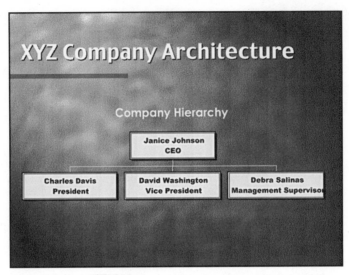

Figure 6-14. Organizational charts are easy to create in PowerPoint and can enhance the information you may want to show about your company.

- When you're finished, click anywhere off the **Datasheet** or slide picture and PowerPoint will return you to your slide. You'll see the finished chart.

Insert an AutoShape:

- From your slide, click **AutoShapes** on the drawing tool-bar.

- Select any of the basic types of shapes offered on the pop-up menu. Then select a specific shape.

- The crosshair pointer tool appears. Use it to click and drag across your slide. The new shape appears. Size it while you're clicking and dragging, or use the **Adjustment Handles** or **Resize Handles** (small boxes that surround the object when it's selected) to change the size and shape of the object (Figure 6-15).

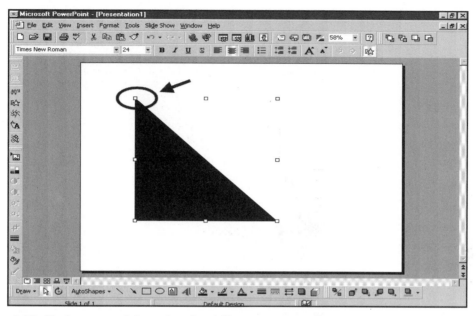

Figure 6-15. Resize artwork by using the **Adjustment Handles** or **Resize Handles**.

Insert clip art:

- Select **New Slide** and choose any **AutoLayout** that shows clip art.

- When the new slide appears, double-click on the **Clip Art** icon. Follow the dialog box instructions to locate the clip art file you want.

- You can preview the clip art pictures, which are usually organized by categories.

- When you find what you like, click once on the picture and click the **Insert** button. Your picture will appear on your slide.

- Use the **Resize Handles** to adjust the size of the art.

- Click and drag the art if you want to move it into a different position.

Insert a photo:

- You can insert scanned photos or pictures from programs other than PowerPoint, provided they exist as files in a folder on your system.

- From **Slide View** go to the **Insert** menu, point to **Picture**, and click **From File** to locate the photo you want.

- A dialog box will appear to help you locate the folder that contains the picture. When you find the picture, double-click on the picture file and it will appear on your slide.

- To insert a photo or artwork you may have just scanned, go to the **Insert** menu, point to **Picture**, and select **From Scanner**.

- The image will appear in an editing program that will allow you to adjust the size, color, or contrast of the artwork before it appears in your PowerPoint slide.

- If you want a certain photo to appear on every slide, go to the **Slide Master** and insert your photo from there.

Insert a logo:

- A logo acts like any other type of art.

- Provided the logo you want is an electronic file in a folder on your system, you can locate it and insert it in a PowerPoint slide.

- Follow the same steps as for "Insert a photo."

- When the logo appears, use the **Resize Handles** to make it the size you want.

- Also, logos are an excellent thing to include on your **Slide Master**. For example, your company logo or your customer's company logo can appear as an art element on every slide in your presentation.

Insert a spreadsheet:

- On the standard toolbar, find the spreadsheet icon (when you roll your cursor over the icon, a small box appears saying "Insert Microsoft Word Excel Worksheet").

- Click the icon, and PowerPoint moves you to an Excel spreadsheet with blank cells. You can use these cells to create the spreadsheet right on the slide.

- When you're finished, click anywhere off the spreadsheet to return to **Slide View**. Your spreadsheet will appear on the new slide.

- Also, you can find an existing spreadsheet and insert it, too. Locate the spreadsheet file, open it, copy it, return to your PowerPoint slide, and paste in the spreadsheet.

Note: For more information on using the appropriate file format for artwork, check your *PowerPoint User's Guide* or click on the **Help** icon from within PowerPoint for more detailed instructions.

Summary

In this chapter you've learned several easy techniques for tightening your copy and making your presentation more visually attractive. If you can write a good, punchy headline for every screen and keep the text simple and large enough to see from a comfortable distance, you'll be far ahead of the crowd in content development.

When it comes to design, allow yourself to be creative. When you combine easy-to-read text with powerful photos or graphics that sell your message, your presentation is bound to attract your customers and focus their attention on your sales information. That's what it's all about!

How to Avoid the Pitfalls in Creating Great-Looking Presentations

Pitfall	*Try This*
My presentation looks too busy.	• Write shorter phrases. Avoid full sentences. • Use only one or two typefonts throughout your presentation. • If you use two fonts, use one for body copy and another for headlines. • Try a simple background color/texture and only one or two other colors for body copy and charts.
It's hard to tell which information is the most important on some of my screens.	• Write a short headline for every screen. • Highlight important information by making it red or some other strong color. • If you have too much information on one screen, break it up into two or three screens.
My presentation seems too long.	• Intersperse key qualifying questions throughout your presentation. • Use one question per screen—in large type.
My presentation seems a little dull. How can I spice it up?	• Think "visual"! A picture is still worth a thousand words. • Use the PowerPoint chart feature to create a simple chart to illustrate a point. • Insert clip art or photos. If you don't have any appropriate photos, ask your marketing department to provide some, or have some taken. Have them scanned as electronic files, and insert them into your show. • Use three to four **WordArt** effects to jazz up your presentation. • Use a single screen to feature a testimonial quote and photo of a satisfied customer. • Incorporate transitions from slide to slide.

Practical Exercises

Exercise 6-1. Launch PowerPoint and open a new blank presentation. Choose a background color and texture that appeals to you. Create 10 new slides (using the **AutoLayouts** of your choices) and write a short headline for each slide. Save your presentation.

Exercise 6-2. Use one of your new slides to practice the chart feature. Use it to build a simple chart that is meaningful to your sales presentation.

Exercise 6-3. Start a different presentation, but this time use one of the preexisting background templates to create your background design.

Exercise 6-4. On the second presentation, find the **Slide Master** and insert a piece of clip art in it. Write your company name in the **Footer** area. Return to **Slide View**. How does it look? Next, create five new slides using these **AutoLayouts**:

- Title slide
- Organizational chart
- Chart (bar chart)
- Table
- Bulleted list

Write a headline for each slide. Create an organizational chart, a bar chart, a table, and a bulleted list. Save your presentation.

• CHAPTER 7 •

The Right Fit: Presentation Types

This chapter offers many suggestions and specific content ideas you might want to use to develop your presentation. In Chapter 5 we talked about getting organized and suggested three possible ways to structure your presentation. In Chapter 6 we looked at the content of several different types of presentations offered in PowerPoint.

In this chapter, we want to take a deeper look at the content and structure of a few common types of sales presentations, including one you might give on an initial call and one that highlights your products and services. We realize that not everything in this section will apply to you or your business. We hope you will pick and choose from ideas that make sense for your situation. If you keep it simple, logically organized, and colorful, you're on your way to creating an excellent sales presentation!

Creating "Initial-Call" Presentations

As a salesperson, the most common presentation you'll give is probably an initial presentation about your company.

Let's say your sales process goes something like this: You've received a sales lead and have already sent out an introductory letter. Your prospect was interested, and you've been able to set up an initial appointment.

In a few days, it's time for your appointment. You've arrived at the site and you're ready to walk through the door and meet your new prospect. It's critical to learn about your prospect's business and establish rapport before using your laptop. Remember, your presentation is only a tool to support your discussion.

When the timing is right, it's very natural for you to move into a brief description of your company, what you're selling, and why others have chosen your products and services. Your job at this natural transition point is to become a storyteller. As we all know, those salespeople who can tell their story in a fun and intriguing way—and even involve the prospect or customer directly in that story—have a far greater chance of succeeding at the overall goal of the sales call—to close the sale!

That's where your laptop computer and a well-designed laptop sales presentation come in. As we have discussed throughout this book, a laptop presentation can help you draw the prospect's attention immediately to your message. It automatically creates interest and excitement. By using it correctly, you can come much closer to your sales goal.

We recommend that you spend only 10 minutes delivering an initial presentation. Design your presentation to focus on four main areas:

1. What is your company all about?
2. What products do you sell or manufacture; what services do you provide?
3. Why are you different or unique?
4. Why do customers like your products and/or services?

The First Purpose of Your Initial Presentation Is to Explain Who You Are and What Your Company Is All About. As you open your laptop and position yourself *shoulder-to-shoulder* with the prospect, you may want to start your initial presentation by showing only two or three content screens.

If your company history is important, you could include a screen that lists a few brief bullet points about history. If your past clients or existing clients have name recognition that can help to build your credibility, consider developing a content screen that lists those clients.

You may be tempted to throw in everything but the kitchen sink, but we strongly recommend that you keep your company overview information to a maximum of two or three content screens. Here are other ideas you could draw from as you write your two-to-three-screen overview:

- Company locations
- Organizational structure—perhaps an organizational chart
- Profiles of corporate officers
- Company strengths, achievements, and awards
- Market position, including comparative statistics on market share and strategic direction

The Second Purpose of Your Initial Sales Presentation Is to Describe in General Terms the Products and Services Your Company Provides. This is not a detailed product presentation. That comes later, perhaps on a second call.

At first, you'll want to give a simple overview that includes some product photos, a few brief bullet-point statements describing your products, and perhaps some text and graphics that will give the prospect a better sense of your company's capabilities. You want to keep this initial presentation pretty broad and avoid getting too detailed at first.

As you briefly show your products and services, consider creating one or two content screens that:

- Display a bullet-point list of your main product families or services
- Or show one or two "beauty shot" color photos of your product line(s) or service(s)
- Or display a tagline that builds confidence—for example, "Ace Marine: Boating's Major Supplier for More Than 30 Years"

The Third Purpose of Your Initial Sales Presentation Is to Answer Why Your Company Is Unique and Why Your Prospect Should Consider What You Have to Offer. Again, keep this part of your presentation to two or three screens and provide a summary of your company's main benefits in short bullet points.

You could also include a testimonial from a satisfied customer. You may want to emphasize your company's reputation for timely response to customers' needs, your 24-hour customer support line, the impeccable quality of your merchandise, your overnight delivery—whatever the key selling points are that characterize your company. Be sure to organize this information in a format that is interesting and easy for a new prospect to understand.

To Close Your Presentation, Consider Including a "Common Questions and Answers" Section to Address the Kinds of Questions That Often Come Up during an Initial Presentation. Those questions might be something like:

- "Why should we consider switching to your company?"
- "What training do you offer to support your products or services?"
- "How can I arrange a demonstration?"
- "What support services are available?"
- "How do you compare with the competition?"
- "How do I contact you if I need help?"

Creating "Product/Service" Presentations

No matter where you are in your sales process, presenting your products or services in detail is a crucial selling step. With interactive laptop presentations, you have a great way to create a colorful, exciting showcase for your products and services.

Consider organizing your product information into four categories. Of course, the information in the following categories can be combined, depending on your company's products and services:

1. Details/features and benefits
2. Applications and uses
3. Technical information
4. Common questions and answers

1. Details/Features and Benefits

As you build the content for this section, you may want to consider the following items:

- Product photos
- Product selection charts
- Cost-comparison charts that show your product against two or three close competitors on important variables
- Options for customizing or personalizing products
- Detailed product information, grouping product families together on one screen or several consecutive screens, including information like this:

  Key features, advantages, and benefits

  Product performance statistics

  Value stories

  Available accessories

  Available colors, sizes, or textures

  Comparisons against competing products

  Warranty information

  Service agreements, options, and packages

  Customer satisfaction reports

  User testimonials

2. Applications and Uses

This is a good section to showcase the typical ways your products and services are used. These applications could be organized by primary and secondary uses, industry, function, or any organizing factor that's appropriate to your market and customers. You might want to include other items like case studies about unusual but successful applications, or instructions for installation, routine care, cleaning, and maintenance. It is also often useful to include applications your customers should avoid.

3. Technical Information

This section can be used for the numbers, test results, and details of your products or services, such as:

- Technical specifications using tables, charts, video or audio clips, and other graphic elements

- Testing methods and results, where applicable
- Comparison data against key competitors
- Compliance to industry standards or regulations
- "Pencil-sell" screens that demonstrate, for example:

   The cost of using your products per application

   The cost of using your products versus your customer's existing method of operation

   How your products save time or money

4. Common Questions and Answers

As with initial-call presentations, you could include answers to common questions in a detailed presentation. For example:

- "What are your payment terms?"
- "What delivery date can I expect?"
- "How will my order be shipped?"
- "Whom do I contact with a question on an order?"
- "What is your return policy?"
- "What is the best way to contact you?"

Creating Other Presentation Types

Flexibility. That's the great thing about learning how to create your own basic presentations. You can be flexible enough to take advantage of new information and new circumstances. For example, if your standard detailed presentation doesn't reflect this quarter's price changes, you don't have to wait for the marketing department to print new flyers. You can quickly build a three-to-five screen PowerPoint show to display new pricing, and even print out the important screens as leave-behinds for your customers to keep.

To allow yourself the maximum flexibility in a sales call, why not create a shorter version of your standard presentation? With both presentations on your laptop, you'll be ready whether you have 5 minutes or 50 minutes with your customer.

Here are a few other types of presentations you can create, along with some ideas about what to include in them.

Advertising Examples. Keep examples of your company's print advertising. Your customers or distributors may be interested in seeing how your company plans to support its new products. Ask your marketing department for the electronic files of print ads, and include them in a brief presentation. You can show TV commercials and play radio spots, too, as long as you can load the electronic files and have the software installed to play them.

Meeting Agendas. Suppose you call a regional meeting, or your distributor wants you to present your new product line to all his sales reps. You can quickly create a meeting agenda and a few accompanying slides specific to the meeting.

Customized Versions of Your Detailed Presentation. These are easy to do in PowerPoint. Call up your standard presentation, do a **Save As**, customize your first screen, go to **Slide Sorter View**, and delete the slides you don't want. Then go to **Slide View**, create any new slides, and resave the new presentation.

Tip: Rename the customized version for your customer's name, so it's easy to remember and find.

Financial Information. Make a separate presentation to showcase the financial information you show most often. It's easy to import your spreadsheets and other data. You can even make spreadsheets directly on your PowerPoint slides.

Marketing Information. Promote your company's Web site by capturing an image of your home page and inserting it into a brief presentation. Include information from the latest press releases, trade show activities, direct mail, and advertising. You can carry the most current sale promotions or special campaigns with you on your laptop by creating a simple presentation.

New Product Development Ideas. Show what's on the drawing board for the coming quarter or the coming year. Combine drawings, mock-ups, and photos with bullet lists of the features, benefits, and unique new features of new products that will soon be available to your customers.

Progress Reports and Status. Summarize your activity with an important client for the past month, six months, year, or range of years.

Summary

In this chapter you have studied two main types of presentations in-depth: (1) initial-call presentations and (2) product/service presentations. For each of these, you have explored the types of content you can include and ways to efficiently organize that content. Besides these main presentation types, you have considered several other kinds of presentations you can develop on your laptop to add to your arsenal of computer-based sales tools.

Armed with *shoulder-to-shoulder* sales skills and a solid presentation or two on your laptop, you should be ready to take your laptop into the field. Now all you need is to become more comfortable hooking up to projection equipment for group presentations, and you'll find some excellent advice on that topic in Chapter 8.

How to Avoid the Pitfalls in Selecting the Right Presentation Type

Pitfall	*Try This*
Sometimes I only get through the first five screens of my standard sales presentation.	• Always have a contingency plan. • Try developing two presentations: a long one (standard) and a short one. Keep both as **Shortcuts** on your **Desktop** screen so they're easy to find. • Choose the best 5–10 screens to combine for a short presentation.
I want to make sure my prospect knows all about my company on our first meeting.	• Think "overview." No need to throw every detail at a prospect during your first call. • Keep your company overview to a maximum of two or three screens. • Stress your company's track record, accomplishments, and one or two key distinguishing factors.
Our client list is impressive, but showing a list on screen isn't very interesting.	• Impress with visuals as well as with name recognition. • Have your clients' logos scanned or obtain the electronic files of the logo artwork. • Insert five or six client logos on one of your presentation screens. If you have more, use two or three screens, but no more than three. • As you talk about your satisfied clients, you can show these logos.
We have an extensive product list. It's tough to pick and choose just a few products to show on an initial call.	• Show categories of products rather than individual products. • Showcase the top two or three best-sellers.

Practical Exercises

Exercise 7-1. On a sheet of paper, write down all the key pieces of information you typically share with a prospect on an initial sales call. How much time do you need to present this information? What key visuals would help you communicate this information?

Exercise 7-2. What kinds of questions come up during an initial presentation? Write those down on a piece of paper. Next, write three bullet-point phrases in answer to each of these questions.

Exercise 7-3. Use the presentation software on your laptop to create a "mini" slide show called "Common Questions and Answers." Make a title slide to that effect. Using one slide per question, put the question first, and then add your answers/solutions in bullet form.

• Part 3 •

Laptop Logistics

CHAPTER 8

Vital Connections: Projectors, LCD Panels, and TVs

Before you start connecting your laptop to anything, it's important to find the right projection equipment for your presentation and to understand a few basics. Three different types of projection systems are available on today's market:

1. *LCD panel.* Liquid crystal display panel that attaches to an overhead projector as a light source. These panels are large, awkward, heavy, and noisy (most have two cooling fans).

2. *LCD projector.* Liquid crystal display with a built-in light source. These systems are quieter, smaller, lighter (some under 10 pounds).

3. *DLP (multimedia) projector.* Digital light processing (DLP) is a technology developed and trademarked by Texas Instruments, although many companies now produce DLP projectors. The system is a self-contained projection unit with its own light source. It does not need to hook up to an overhead projector. It can be quite heavy—up to 40 pounds or more. Lots of functionality with these systems. Also pricey. The good news is that the size, weight, and price of DLP systems are coming down.

Projector Issues. Consider these issues before dusting off your credit card to buy that expensive projection system:

- *How is the equipment going to be used?* On sales calls? Mostly for group presentations? Lots of travel?

- *How many people in your office will use the equipment?* Assess the demand. Maybe you'll need two or three projection systems.

- *Can all your users handle the weight of the system, especially when they travel?* Projection systems range from about 10 pounds to more than 40 pounds. The hard-sided travel case can add 25 pounds of additional weight, and the system is very bulky. It's too big for the overhead bins on an airplane, and therefore must be checked.

- *What level of brightness do you need?* Brightness is given in terms of lumens. In general, higher-light environments require brighter projectors. Top-of-the-line projectors have a grayscale brightness of 1200 lumens. The highest color brightness available is 800 lumens. Also, LCD-type projectors cannot project as bright an image as DLP-type projectors.

- *What type of projector lamp is appropriate for your use?* Two types of lamps are typical: metal halide lamps (last from 1000 to 3000 hours, but require a heavy transformer, cost hundreds of dollars, and may need a technician to change them) and halogen lamps (last only 40 to 70 hours, but you can change them yourself).

- *What types of computers will connect to the projection system?* All Macs? All PCs? A mix of both?

- *What about image resolution and clarity?* Can the projector you can afford handle your laptop's resolution? The high-end projectors on the market have something called "intelligent compression" and a top available resolution of 1024×768 XGA. If your presentation calls for high resolution (true 800×600 or 1024×768), your best bet is an LCD panel. The panel device hooks to your laptop and then sits on top of a regular overhead projector. The panel systems offer higher resolution that's not available with an LCD panel projector (self-contained unit with its own light source) or most DLP projection systems. There are high-end DLP projectors designed to handle 1024 × 768 resolution, but they're prohibitively expensive and therefore not widely available as rentals.

- *Will your presentations incorporate video clips or VHS videos?* Do you need output to a VCR? Two VCRs?

- *Do you need the projector to hook to multiple laptops?* Not all projectors offer dual-monitor connections.

- *Do you need really good speakers?* It depends on how big the presentation room will be. Newer projectors have built-in stereo-quality sound that's good enough to be heard in a large meeting room. Others require a connection to the site's sound system to produce enough volume to be heard. Still others do not allow you to plug into outside speakers.

- *Do you need a projection system that automatically adjusts its settings to match your laptop's image size, synchronization, tracking, and other settings?* The higher-end machines will do this for you through features called **Auto Resize** and **Auto Image.** They'll search your laptop for the measurements that control its image resolution. Lower-end projectors have to be programmed to these settings by hand, which could be an issue for your company if many people with different-model laptops will be using the projection system.

- *How much can you afford to spend?* Projection systems range from $1900 to $10,000.

Preparation and Setup

Connecting your laptop to a projector, LCD panel, or TV is definitely easier than programming a VCR. Once you have done it, you'll be very comfortable with the process.

Before You Arrive

Before you arrive at the meeting, you'll want to request a conference room that has a projection screen, plenty of space, and preferably no windows. If windows are present, make sure there are blinds or shades that can be drawn. If not, request another room where sunlight won't be a problem. In addition, look for lights that dim versus fluorescent lights that just switch on and off.

Always prepare handouts to give to meeting attendees. Consider creating an agenda for the meeting, printing it out, and making copies before you arrive on site. This shows you're prepared and organized. Also, bring copies of any brochures you want to use as leave-behinds.

Making Vital Connections

You have three choices for obtaining a projection system: Bring your own, rent it locally, or use the customer's projection system, if one is available on-site. Of course, you'll be more comfortable and have more control over the setup if you bring your own projection equipment. But good rental equipment is readily available from local audiovisual rental houses. If you are going to rent, be sure to call ahead to make a reservation, especially when your presentation is out of town.

You have three equipment options.

1. *LCD panels.* The first option is to use an LCD panel that sits on top of an overhead projector. LCD panels have good resolution, and they're easy to use, but they depend on the brightness of the overhead projector's bulb to beam an image onto the screen

2. *Multimedia projectors.* The second option is a multimedia projector that has its own light source that shines up on the screen. Compared with LCD panels, these are clearly superior in screen brightness. These typically sit on the conference table, have great image quality, and are also easy to use. There are many different brands, including those from 3M, In-Focus, CTX, and Dukane.

3. *Connect to a TV.* The third option is to connect your laptop to a TV using a converter box or using a "TV-OUT" port on the back of your laptop. Even though the picture

may not be as crisp, a TV is typically available in most conference rooms.

Connecting to LCD Panels

First, place the LCD panel on the overhead projector and then place your laptop fairly close to the overhead projector. Plug all three items into a power strip, *but don't turn them on yet.*

Second, look for a port on the back of your laptop that has 15 holes or pins. Then connect a 15-pin cord that comes with the LCD panel to the back of your Windows laptop. Next connect the other end to a similar port on the LCD panel. If you're using a Mac laptop, the procedure is the same, but the cord may need an adapter.

The Turn-On Sequence Is Pretty Important. Turn the LCD panel on first, then turn on the overhead projector, and, last, turn on your laptop. This sequence ensures that your laptop will "sense" that a projector has been connected so it will project an image on the screen.

Most newer laptops will have a **Function** key that allows you to toggle back and forth between displaying only on your laptop screen, displaying only on the projection screen, or displaying on both screens simultaneously. By holding down the **Function** key and pressing the appropriate "F" key, you can toggle between these three options. We recommend using a simultaneous display so you have the most control over viewing your presentation.

Keep in mind, if you want to hook up a VCR or your laptop's sound system to either an LCD panel or a multimedia projector, it's easy to plug it into the appropriate input jacks. The benefit is better sound quality and the ability to project a video onto the screen from a VCR.

Fine-Tuning. Now that you can see your desktop projected up on the screen, take the time to focus the overhead projector to make it clear. Additionally, you can adjust the horizontal and vertical alignment by pressing the appropriate buttons on the panel or the remote control.

Connecting to Multimedia Projectors

First, position the projector about 15 to 20 feet from your projection screen. Then position your laptop at a convenient location toward the front of the room and plug in the projector and your laptop into a power strip, but *don't turn them on yet.* Just like on an LCD panel, connect the 15-pin cord to both your laptop and the projector.

Important: Turn on the projector first, wait a few seconds, and then turn on your laptop.

Keep in mind, most projectors have a **Standby** button. If you don't see an image on the screen after the projector has warmed up, you may need to press the **Standby** button to turn on the light source.

Also, the **Standby** button is a great feature. Let's say you're in the middle of your presentation and you want to turn up the lights for a brief Q&A session. You can push the **Standby** button and the screen your audience sees will go blank. When you're ready to resume, push the **Standby** button again and you're right back to where you were, ready to go.

In addition, there may be a **Blank** button on the remote control. This will also turn the image on the screen "off and on" to refocus the group's attention on you.

Again, you can use the **Function** keys to toggle through the three options to simultaneously show your image on the screen and on your laptop display.

Fine-Tuning. After you're set up, you're ready to complete all your fine-tuning adjustments. You can adjust the legs on the front and back to center the light source on the screen. Also, you can zoom in or out to increase or decrease the size of your image.

To focus the projector you typically use the remote control or buttons on the projector. And, like before, you can adjust the horizontal and vertical alignment, along with brightness, contrast, and other settings, by using the remote control or buttons located on the projector.

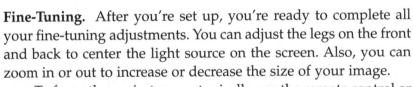

Connecting to a TV

It's easy to hook your laptop to a TV, provided you buy a converter box that will convert your laptop presentation into a format that can be displayed using a TV set as a monitor. Check with your local electronics or computer store.

To hook up your laptop, connect one side of the cord to the converter box and the other end to the 15-pin port on your laptop. Then connect one end of the video cable to the converter box and the other end to the "video in" port on the TV. Next, connect the power cord to the converter box and to a wall socket. Now start your computer and launch your presentation; you should see it on the TV. As before, you can adjust the horizontal and vertical alignment.

Final Preparation

Before your meeting, be sure to launch your presentation and check to make sure the sound is adjusted and the show looks good on the display screen. Keep in mind, if you do have problems, begin with the owner's manual for the projector. If that doesn't help, try the manufacturer's 800 number or call a local A/V rental house. Someone at either of these places can typically troubleshoot problems over the phone.

Next, tape down your power cords with duct tape so they're not a safety hazard.

If you have customized the first screen of your presentation for your meeting, display that screen as your attendees gather.

Summary

In this chapter you have explored some issues to consider when selecting the right projection equipment for your presentation. Also, you were introduced to three options for projection equipment: LCD panels, multimedia projectors, and connecting to a TV for display output.

By design, our instructions have been simple rather than detailed for two reasons. The first is to show you that it's quite easy to connect to this equipment and that you have every reason to feel confident about this process. Secondly, we realize that every piece of equipment is going to be somewhat different. Your best bet is to read the user's manual and to practice with the equipment until you are fully comfortable connecting your laptop and displaying your presentation in front of a group.

How to Avoid the Pitfalls in Connecting to Projectors, LCD Panels, and TVs

Pitfall	Try This
Not enough electrical outlets.	• Always bring your own power strip and extension cord(s).
My presentation is displaying on the projection screen, but it doesn't look right.	• Your projector or LCD panel could be set to a different screen resolution than your computer. The higher-end systems will automatically make them the same through **Auto Resize** and **Auto Image**. If you don't have a high-end projector, you'll have to set the screen resolution manually. • For example, your projector might be set to a screen resolution of 1024 × 768 pixels, while your laptop is set to 800 × 600 pixels. • Try resetting them so they match. • From your **Desktop** screen, go to the **Start** button, choose **Settings**, then **Control Panel**, then **Display**. In the **Display Properties** dialog box, select on the **Settings** tab to adjust the resolution and colors on your laptop.
The projector is on, but no image displays.	• Try pressing the **Standby** button on the projector. • Or find the **Function** key on your laptop that toggles from a blank screen to an image. Try that key until you see an image.
In the middle of my presentation, the projection screen sometimes goes blank.	• Make sure your laptop hasn't gone to sleep. Move your mouse or touchpad to wake up the system. • Is the image still on your laptop? Try the **Function** key toggle to resend input to the projector. • Hit the **Input** button on the remote control to resend the image to the projector. • Try restarting your laptop as you continue your presentation. • Call a break in the meeting to allow you to troubleshoot. • *Worst-case scenario:* The projector bulb may be burned out. Typically, you won't have access to another bulb. Ask for another projector. Or if you own the projector, carry an extra bulb with you.

How to Avoid the Pitfalls in Connecting to Projectors, LCD Panels, and TVs (*Cont.*)

Pitfall	Try This
Sometimes I want to pause my presentation, but shutting down my laptop and rebooting is too awkward.	• The best way is to use the **Blank** option on your remote control to make the screen image stop and reset quickly. • Also, you can use the **Standby** feature. • Another way is to place the projector lens cap over the lens as you conduct a discussion. Then take it off when you're ready to proceed.
The projection display is cutting off part of my **Desktop** screen.	• Adjust the vertical or horizontal alignment on the projector. • You may have to manually shift the projector to make sure you can display the portion of the screen you want to display.
I have trouble using the projector remote control.	• Once your laptop is properly connected to the projector or LCD panel, turn on the equipment. • Adjust (align) the horizontal and vertical controls on the projector and remote. • Use the focus control and the zoom to adjust the image. • Be sure your laptop and projection equipment are set to the same resolution.
I run into volume problems when I try to connect my laptop to the audio system on the projector.	• Carry the right connector cords with you. • Bring the right jacks—usually a mini jack (stereo preferred) connecting to an RCA male plug. • Or mini jack to mini jack. • Try turning your laptop volume all the way up first before adjusting the volume on the projection unit. • *Option:* Carry a small set of speakers with you.

Practical Exercises

Exercise 8-1. Depending on the availability of the equipment, practice connecting your laptop to an LCD panel. Find the setting to display your presentation on the projection screen only. Next, find the setting that will display your presentation on both your laptop and the projection screen. Toggle back and forth until you're comfortable.

Exercise 8-2. Depending on availability of the equipment, practice connecting your laptop to a multimedia projector. Display your presentation on-screen. Locate and activate the **Standby** button. Then deactivate **Standby**.

Exercise 8-3. Find the appropriate connection cords and jacks to plug your laptop's audio function into the multimedia projector's sound system or the sound system that may be in place in the conference room or training room.

Exercise 8-4. Depending on availability of the equipment, practice connecting your laptop to a TV and using the TV as your presentation display screen. What do you notice about the resolution of your presentation when you show it on a TV screen rather than with an LCD panel or multimedia projector?

• CHAPTER 9 •

Your Laptop: The Communications Connection

Your laptop is your communications connection, no matter where you are or what time it is. With your laptop, the right software and hardware, and a little know-how, you'll be connected to your colleagues and to your customers and prospects. Also, you'll be connected to the Internet and begin to discover the power of specific information that will help you advance your sales process.

In this chapter you'll find out about how to access the Internet and use some of the sales applications available to you online. You'll also become familiar with some commonsense ways to use e-mail more effectively and to your advantage with customers. And finally, you'll learn how to start carrying less paper and more information with you on your sales calls.

Becoming "Web-Wise"

You can access the Internet from any location if you have a computer, a modem, a Web browser, an account with an Internet service provider (ISP), and an 800 number or local number, which most services provide.

What is the Internet? Good question. A few basic definitions are in order:

- *The Internet.* A collection of computer networks linked all over the world via a series of local-area networks (LANs) and wide-area networks (WANs), through which information is shared. The Internet began with the U.S. government in the early 1960s with just four major computers. It has grown from those four "hosts" to 2300 host computers in 1986 to millions of host computers and tens of millions of individual users today.

121

- *World Wide Web.* Basically, the Web amounts to software sitting on the Internet that makes it easier for users to access information. The Web is a huge collection of Web sites, or individual addresses through which users can locate specific information.

- *Internet service provider.* An ISP is your means to connect to the World Wide Web portion of the Internet. You pay an ISP—just like you pay the phone company or the gas company—for a service. That service amounts to access for the right phone number(s) and a password to keep your connection secure. Some ISPs have a wider offering, including an e-mail program, a Web browser, and a file transfer protocol (FTP), a standard process by which you access the files and programs available on the Internet.

- *Online service provider.* An online service provider is like an ISP, but with more in-depth content and services exclusive to that provider (like America Online or CompuServe). Such providers produce and/or gather large stores of information on news, weather, sports, business, health, and many other topics. Plus they offer extensive online customer support.

- *Web browser.* The Web browser is more software that acts like a means of transportation among the many sites on the Web. It also serves as the GUI, or graphical user interface, between the humans that want information and the electronic bits and bytes that live on the Internet. Internet Explorer is the Windows built-in Web browser, but you can use others.

OK, so now you're connected, but of what use is the Internet to a salesperson? What information can you find on the Internet that you can actually use to help you sell? The answer is, a lot. If you know what to look for and how to target your search, you can uncover a great deal of extremely useful information on the Internet to help you make the sale. Here are a few ideas for starters:

Use the Internet for preparation. Study your customers' Web sites—do your homework on new prospects. Research the relevant facts and figures, and walk into your sales call armed with current information.

Keep up on the competitors' products and services. Be aware of their pricing, latest offers, even news of contracts they may publish on the Web.

Read newspapers and magazines online. Keep up on the trade journals in your industry.

Tailor your laptop to gather news on keywords you specify. For example, you can set your Web browser to search for recent articles on a current customer's company or on a firm you would like to prospect. The system will search for keywords, gather abstracts or full articles, and download these to a file you can check whenever you want.

Show your own Web site on a call. Your company's own Web site is an excellent sales tool to show on your laptop computer. Before you try this, however, practice connecting your laptop in various environments until you feel confident about accessing your Web site. The relative stability of your laptop as well as many other uncontrollable factors can eat up precious *shoulder-to-shoulder* sales time. Be sure you can access your Web site with ease before attempting it live during a call.

Another technique is to capture your Web site's home page as a single image (ask your marketing department to provide this). Then you use it as a "map" to show customers what they will find on your Web site if they want to explore it on their own time.

Accessing the Internet

The Internet is available to you through your laptop wherever you travel. All you need is a modem, a telephone cord, an RJ-11 single-line phone jack (typical telephone jack), and a local access number.

Your Internet service provider has the local numbers for the cities and towns where you travel. You can set them by entering the appropriate area code in your ISP setup area and choosing from among a list of local numbers.

Tip: Choose local numbers in advance for the places you travel to often. If you travel to San Francisco frequently, for example, you can set up Internet access numbers for San Francisco from your home base. You don't have to wait until you're in the City by the Bay to find a local number for Internet access.

Faxing a Document from Your Laptop

You can use your laptop to fax any document you have in electronic form. In general, you'll require the following items to fax from your laptop:

- A built-in fax modem or a PCMCIA fax/modem card.
- An RJ-11 telephone jack on the laptop.
- A telephone cord to connect from the laptop to the wall jack.
- Fax software—Windows 95, Windows 98, and Windows NT have fax software built into the Microsoft Exchange program. Or you can purchase fax software separately.

To Send or Receive a Fax from the Office, Hotel, or Home. As long as you have a fax/modem and can connect your laptop to a telephone wall jack, you can send or receive a fax from within any Windows application. To do this, use the **Print** command and select **Fax** as your printer option for the document you want to fax.

Or you can use the Microsoft Exchange software to send and receive faxes. Activate Microsoft Exchange by double-clicking on the **Inbox** icon on your **Desktop**.

- To send a fax from Microsoft Exchange, go to the **Compose** menu and select **New Fax**. Follow the instructions in the **Compose New Fax** wizard dialog box.

- To receive a fax through Microsoft Exchange, go to the **Tools** menu, point to **Microsoft Fax Tools**, and choose **Request a Fax**. Follow the instructions in the **Request a Fax** wizard dialog box.

To Send a Fax from Your Cell Phone. This process is a bit more complicated. You'll need the following items:

- An electronic document ready to fax

- A data-capable cell phone (currently, most of Motorola's cellular phones are data-capable; about half of the Nokia models are data-capable; almost none of the Erickson cell phones is data-capable)

- A cell-ready fax/modem (either built into your laptop or on a PCMCIA card)

- The proper cable with an adapter to connect the laptop to a cell phone

- A strong cellular signal

- Another computer or fax machine to receive the fax

It is possible, given the above items, to fax a document from your cell phone. You should know, however, that the package with a cell-ready modem, cable, and adapter runs around $500, in addition to the cost of a data-capable cell phone. Also, because the technology is somewhat behind in this area, the transmission speed of your fax is limited to 3200 bps (bits per second), which is quite slow.

You may want to try faxing one-page thank-you letters from your cell phone, provided you meet the hardware and software requirements. But send your longer faxes from a regular phone connection at the hotel, office, or home.

Managing E-mail Madness

Electronic messaging, or e-mail, is one of the laptop features salespeople use most. It's also the most widely used function in connecting to the Internet for both business users and home users.

E-mail is great, but all too quickly it can become over-whelming. In this section, you'll learn about e-mail, how to use it, and some good tips for how to manage it so that it works to your advantage.

A Few E-mail Facts

According to a 1999 study out of John Carroll University in Cleveland, the use of e-mail in the United States alone is increasing at a rate of 20 percent per year. One hundred million Americans are now using e-mail to send three billion messages every year.

As a result, e-mail has now become ubiquitous in American society. You can send and receive messages not only from your office computer and from virtually any location with your laptop, but from kiosks at trade shows, from booths at coffee houses (so-called Internet cafés), and even from the treadmills at your local health club.

The Upside. E-mail has been called the great equalizer. Because communications are instant and access is universal—particularly in e-mail-oriented companies—organizations that were previously hierarchical have now begun to flatten out. Workers at all levels can communicate with top corporate officers in a way that was never possible before.

Studies have also found that in the daily work world, people are away from their desks 75 percent of the time. And they now respond less often to phone calls than to e-mail. In fact, if workers are at their computers and see that they have a new e-mail message, they feel a sense of urgency and curiosity to read the new message and respond. They feel less urgency when it comes to the telephone.

People enjoy e-mail for many reasons. One of the benefits of e-mail is the ability to save important messages. These provide a record of correspondence as well as an electronic "paper trail" that can become important in complex projects or negotiations.

In fact, 50 percent of the work today is interactive. International teams can now work across time zones, gaining efficiencies because of e-mail that were impossible 10 or 15 years ago. The time of day people work is becoming less important. Work can be accomplished in any location at any hour, and the necessary communication can take place instantly around the clock through e-mail.

Another upside: E-mail demands brevity. Long messages have become far less acceptable as the volume of messages increases.

The Downside. It's easy, it's quick, it's cheap, but often it's too much. The average worker now receives between 15 and 50 electronic messages a day. Many of these are unnecessary or simply junk mail. New software can help filter "spam," or unwanted messages, but these programs are not yet 100 percent reliable. There are too many variables.

Another risk: Handling e-mail can become almost addictive, which may lead to another risk—the mistaken belief that hours spent reading and responding to e-mail are productive. E-mail can be productive if it's managed well, but often it simply eats time. Also, the sheer volume of e-mail messages has become an additional and significant stress factor for many workers.

Awareness is the key. Even given the disadvantages of e-mail, you can still learn to capitalize on its advantages and make it work in your favor.

Using E-mail

Chances are, you are set up and comfortable using e-mail already. If not, you need to know a few basics.

To send an e-mail message you need a computer, a modem, and an account with an Internet service provider. Generally, your company will already have an ISP and its own preferred messaging system.

If you need to establish e-mail capability, contact an ISP (such as America Online, CompuServe, or many other providers) and follow the provider's instructions. Local access providers are listed in the Yellow Pages.

You'll need to receive and load some communications software that may be specific to your provider. As well, you'll need to follow the installation and registration instructions on the packaging and documentation.

Once you are set up with an ISP, sending an e-mail message is easy. All you need is the e-mail address of the person you want to contact. Follow the on-screen prompts or printed instructions with your communications software.

E-mail Courtesy

As a salesperson, ongoing communication with your customers is extremely important. Be proactive and find out your customer's preferred method of communication with you. As you close an initial sales call with a new prospect, find out if that person prefers voice mail or e-mail contact with you. When you respect the communication method your customer prefers, he or she is more likely to respond to you in a positive way.

If your customer prefers to receive e-mail, consider using your laptop to send a thank-you e-mail message just minutes or hours following the call. If the customer prefers a fax, then fax a thank-you note from your car, the airport, or your office. If it's regular mail, use one of the business letter templates on your laptop and send a formal letter on letterhead.

If you elect to communicate with your customers via e-mail, your messages stand a better chance of receiving a timely response if you learn to use a little basic e-mail courtesy. Here are a few e-mail tips:

- Make sure you have the correct e-mail address for the intended receiver of your message.
- Label e-mail messages with a good subject description—something your intended receiver can use to determine whether he or she must respond to your message right away.
- Make the e-mail message brief and succinct.
- If you are sending an attached file, use your "cover" message to give the filename as well as the program and version used to create it. Also give some indication of the file's length or size. In your cover message, you could

say, for example: "I'm attaching a 57-screen PowerPoint 97 file named 'present.ppt' with this e-mail."

- Avoid sending the same message to a group of people. Your customer can tell when any message is not intended specifically for him or her. If the message is important enough to send, customize it for each receiver.

- If you want your receiver to do something specific, provide a clear statement of these action steps.

- Avoid sending jokes or unnecessary information. Not everyone's sense of humor is the same, and you risk a turn-off. Plus these have become time wasters, which your customers may resent.

Making E-mail Work to Your Sales Advantage

When you *send* e-mail, you can make the process a lot easier by keeping these simple ideas in mind:

- *Keep an address book.* You'll save yourself a lot of typing. Most online services provide this feature. You can highlight and copy the e-mail address of anyone who sends you a message. Some address books do this for you automatically. Click on your address book button and paste the address in the appropriate field. Then type in the first and last name of the person, and you're done.

  The next time you need to correspond with that person, all you have to do is open your address book and click on the name, and the correct e-mail address will appear on your message. You can manually add names to the address book at any time. You can delete or edit addresses, too.

- *Use caution in general.* Be aware that your e-mail messages are not necessarily confidential. It's possible for them to be read by anyone who has access to the receiver's computer. The receiver can also elect to forward your message to anyone and everyone.

- *Use extra caution when dealing with sensitive material.* Be careful about sending confidential or sensitive material via e-mail for the same reasons as above.

- *Compress large files.* If you're attaching a large file, it's a good idea to compress it first so that it will download more quickly on the other end. Common compression programs, like Disk-Doubler or Stuff-It, may already reside on your laptop. If not, check with your MIS department or local computer store. Also, many e-mail programs will automatically compress your attachments.

When you *receive* e-mail, try these techniques to simplify this process:

- Check your e-mail every day whenever possible. Avoid letting messages pile up.

- Set a certain time of day to go through your e-mail. Unless you are expecting an urgent message or file, try to stick to your established time. Also, set a time limit, say 30 minutes, for handling e-mail each day.

- Let the people with whom you frequently communicate know that you check messages at a certain time of day. If they need you more urgently, ask them to call you.

- As you check your list of e-mail, scan the subject lines. Delete anything you're sure is junk mail. You can delete it without having to read it.

- Next, read the important messages. Take a moment for a quick reply, if a reply is warranted.

- Save important messages to a folder on your hard disk. After they're saved, delete these messages from your mailbox.

- Read through the rest of your messages, responding only to those that warrant a response and deleting as many as you can.

- Get in the habit of handling your e-mail messages now rather than later. Read them, save the important ones to another folder, and clean the rest out of your mailbox.

- Or you may want to print any messages that need study or more thought on your part. Take the printouts with you.

Techniques for Controlling Junk E-mail

As the Internet has become more popular and more widely used, so has junk e-mail. Use these commonsense tips to help control the amount of spam you receive:

- Realize that your activities in the public aspects of the Internet can expose you to greater risk of receiving junk e-mail. These activities might include joining online mailing lists (to receive information on a topic of interest), participating in chat rooms, posting on message boards or newsgroups, or creating a Web page under your name.

- Learn to recognize junk mail. Scan the subject lines. Look at the sender's address. Is it one you recognize?

- Don't give away your password or credit card number to people who ask for it online.

- Don't reply to junk e-mail, even if you see an option to reply if you want to be removed from the mailing list. This is a way for junk e-mailers to confirm that you have received and read the message—and to confirm your current e-mail address.

- Avoid downloading files or clicking on hyperlinked text (underlined words that link to other Web sites) that may appear on e-mail from someone you don't know. Downloading strange files and clicking hyperlinks are a good way to pick up an unwanted virus that can damage your system.

- Use the e-mail controls provided by your online service or Internet service provider. You can block specific screen names, Internet addresses, or mail from certain domains. You can even block the exchange of attached files or pictures that come with e-mail messages.

- Use the e-mail controls to set your system to accept only those messages from a list of addresses you build, you control.
- Notify your e-mail service provider if you are getting too much spam. These services are responding aggressively to member complaints and have begun to actively pursue and successfully prosecute spammers.

Carry Less Paper/More Information

You have a terrific computer-based sales presentation to showcase your products and services, and you've won the opportunity to present it to a new prospect. On that type of call, what are you trying to accomplish specifically?

Initially, you're there to explore options and products that could interest your prospect. You're questioning, listening, and learning—and providing technical information about products. You could be comparing and contrasting different products within your own line, or comparing your products against your competitor's line. You're pressing to come back with a proposal, or to close the sale right then if your prospect is ready to buy on the spot.

With the presentations and information set up thoughtfully in advance of your call, you stand a good chance of using your laptop to show some of your most persuasive information:

- Material safety data sheets (MSDS)
- Scanned images of your printed sales support materials
- Product photos
- Price sheets
- Technical specifications
- Product catalogs
- Cost comparisons among several products or between your products and the competitor's line
- Features and benefits
- Detailed schematics

- Printed, audio, or video testimonials from satisfied customers
- Competitive information

It's a good idea to load your frequently used sales support material (spec sheets, feature/benefits charts, cost-comparison charts, "pencil-sell" worksheets, price lists, product photos) onto your laptop. Learn how to organize them so you can access them quickly during a sales call. This is one of the most powerful sales techniques you can use to your advantage on your laptop.

Here are a few details about how you can carry less paper on your sales calls as you begin to carry more and more useful information on your laptop computer.

Show Comparisons between Products. Prospects often want to know the difference in features and benefits of one product versus another. Computer-based presentations are superb for this type of comparison.

Select at least two products that are often compared. Then identify several variables on which to compare them. Create a chart (or ask that one be created) to list the products and the data for each variable in such a way that your customers can see at a glance the similarities and differences among products.

Keep Relevant Competitive Information under a Generic Filename. It's obviously important to know your competition. Although we do not recommend talking about your competitors during a sales call, we realize that sometimes you may need to show this type of information, especially if you work in a highly competitive arena.

You may want to collect information on your competitor in a separate, easily accessible file on your **Desktop**. It's a good idea to label the file something other than "Competitive Information." Think of a separate generic filename understood by you, but one that your prospects could not guess. Our experience is that when others look at your **Desktop** screen, they look at everything on your screen, no matter what's on it. If they see something labeled "Competitive Information," they will ask you about it.

Organize Your Main Presentations by Separate, Independent Sections for Flexibility. Suppose you don't have an advanced presentation with pathways branching off a main menu. All you have is a PowerPoint-type linear presentation. You can achieve the same effect as if you had an advanced presentation by organizing your basic presentation into a few "mini" presentations on your **Desktop** and creating **Shortcuts** to each one of them.

Maybe these mini presentations are only four or five PowerPoint screens' worth of information each. One mini show could be labeled "Company Overview"; a second show could be labeled "Products and Services"; a third, "Specifications"; a fourth, "Customer Service"; a fifth, "Ordering Information"; a sixth, "Common Questions and Answers"; and so on. To achieve this, open your main presentation. Go to **Slide Sorter View** in PowerPoint, select a range of slides, and then use **Copy** and **Paste** to paste them into a new presentation file and save them under a different filename.

Include External Resources. Your laptop allows you to keep a file of resources (in print or as audio/video testimonials) that support your sales presentation.

Read the trade publications for your industry and clip relevant articles. Pick out statistics, charts, and quotations that support your product lines, your ideas, and your company's strategic direction. Collect favorable news about your clients and prospects. Scan these and store them in an easily accessed file on your **Desktop**. Click on these at appropriate times during the sales call to support your position, add to the discussion, or answer a prospect's questions. You can also use the Internet to find and download material you may want to show on your laptop.

Scan Support Materials to Create PDF Files in Adobe Acrobat. The laptop gives you the power to capture and display technical data sheets, business cards, and most support materials just as they appear in printed form. By scanning your brochures and data sheets, you can create portable document files (PDF) that you can show to a customer using Adobe Acrobat software.

You'll need a scanner and a copy of Adobe Acrobat. To scan a photo, text page, or printed material (one page at a time):

- Read your scanner user's manual for setup instructions.

- Cable the scanner to your laptop by following the setup instructions that come with the scanner.

- Turn the scanner on and launch its resident software program, which will appear on your laptop screen.

- Place the item you want to scan face down on the scanner (for flatbed types) or insert the document according to your user's manual (for handheld, sheetfed, slide, or drum style scanners).

- Click the **Preview** button, which causes the scanner to capture the image and display it on your laptop screen.

- From here you can crop the image electronically and choose the size and resolution you desire. If the item will be viewed only on screen, it can be scanned at low resolution (72 dots per inch), which will not take up so much memory on your system.

- Click the **Scan** button on your screen. The scanner will perform a detailed scan of the image, which can take from a few seconds to several minutes to complete.

- The image pops back onto your screen as an untitled file. Now save the image as a PDF.

- Once saved, you can open your PDF scan file from within the Adobe Acrobat program.

Take a Portable Printer with You. Some salespeople are now traveling with highly portable, lightweight printers to give them the flexibility of printing information before, during, or after a sales call. Visit your local computer store and ask for a demonstration.

Summary

This chapter has provided a lot of detail about ways you can use your laptop as a full-service communication connection to your colleagues, customers, and prospects. You know how to access the Internet and find the types of information that can give you the competitive edge in your sales process.

By completing the exercises at the end of this chapter, you may discover for yourself that the Internet is a vast collection of information. Each journey into this extraordinary pool of information is an individual experience. A single Web site can take hours to explore. Every visit to the same site can be different, depending on the links you click. Every hyperlink leads somewhere else, in turn.

The value you gain from the Internet is a personal effort. Use "bookmarks" to leave a trail of breadcrumbs that will quickly lead you back to the best, most useful places you find on your journey.

Whatever information you can store on your laptop can be transmitted to your customers via fax and e-mail. You have learned a few useful facts about e-mail and faxing that will help you connect and stay in touch with customers from anywhere you have access to a telephone.

This chapter has also provided specifics about more effective ways to capture and show sales information from your laptop. As you begin to try some of these information techniques, we feel certain you'll want more and more sales tools on your laptop to add to your arsenal of sales ammunition.

How to Avoid the Pitfalls in Connecting and Communicating with Your Laptop

Pitfall	Try This
I find good Web sites, but don't always write down the address. If the address is complicated, sometimes it's difficult to find that site again.	• Use the **bookmark** or **favorite places** feature on your Web browser. • When you're on the Web page, go to your toolbar and look for the **bookmark** feature. One or two clicks here will save the Web site address on a list of your favorite places. • Next time you're online, go back to **bookmarks** on the toolbar and click on the address you want. The browser will immediately connect to the Internet and go directly to that site. • Also, most browsers will let you arrange your favorite sites into folders to keep them well organized and easy to find.
I get more than 15 e-mails every day. I'm distracted by trying to answer each one as it comes in.	• Check your e-mail messages once a day. Set one particular time of day to read and respond to them. • Stick to this time of day. Let others know about it. • Limit the time you use to handle e-mail. Try to complete your e-mail in a maximum of 30 minutes.
I'm starting to get a lot of spam e-mails.	• Notify your online service provider. • Avoid responding to spam messages in any way. • Follow the procedures outlined by your service provider to decrease the number of unwanted messages you receive.
I have a good computer-based presentation, but find myself relying on printed brochures during a sales call.	• Maybe the presentation you have doesn't work for you. • Try creating a new PowerPoint presentation yourself that summarizes key points from your printed material. • Scan, or ask to have scanned, the most useful elements from your printed materials. • Drop these into your new PowerPoint presentation. • Use your brochure as a "leave-behind," and use your laptop computer as your primary presentation tool.

Practical Exercises

Exercise 9-1. Assuming you have access to the Internet, try this exercise. On a piece of paper, list three to five major periodicals you read routinely for news of your industry or for business news in general. See if you can find a Web site for each of them on the Internet. Bookmark these sites so you can quickly return to them in the future. On any of these sites, find one current, full-text article that relates to a problem or concern you may be experiencing. Practice printing it.

Exercise 9-2. Using a letter that you create fresh or one already filed on your laptop, practice faxing it from your laptop at home to the fax machine at your office. Or try faxing a test letter directly from your laptop to a friend's fax machine. Did you have any problems with the fax? What additional information do you need to successfully complete the fax of an electronic document from your laptop to a dedicated fax machine?

Exercise 9-3. Assuming you have an online service with e-mail, go to the e-mail feature on your system and start an address book. Enter four or five e-mail addresses of people you communicate with routinely. If you have already established an address book for e-mail, take a few moments to open it and edit any addresses that may be incorrect or delete those that are no longer relevant.

Exercise 9-4. If you have a basic PowerPoint presentation on your laptop, use the procedures in this chapter to break it into three or four mini presentations under different filenames. Create a **Desktop Shortcut** to each.

Exercise 9-5. If you have access to a scanner, try scanning a single page from one of your printed sales brochures. Choose one with a photo, a chart, or a graphic. Follow the procedure outlined in this chapter for scanning a document. Once you have completed the scan, named the image, and filed the scan in a folder on your laptop, try opening PowerPoint and starting a blank presentation. Select a template that allows you to add artwork, and drop your scan into the slide. Size it and move it around until it looks good. Write two or three descriptive bullets next to the scan to explain the information. Save your work. Use it to build a new basic sales presentation.

• Part 4 •

User Tips and Tools

CHAPTER 10

Tips and Templates for Writing Letters and Proposals

As a salesperson, you require a number of documents and templates to support your day-to-day sales activity. The laptop computer gives you a wide range of sales tools at your fingertips, including letters, e-mail messages, faxes, and presentations on diskette.

About Sales Letters. Good sales letters are some of the easiest things to create on a laptop. The hardest part is writing a good letter. If you create one that works, you can use it over and over again. It's a smart idea to create a bank of frequently used letters.

About Templates. A template is a pattern for something. With your laptop you have the power to create templates for proposals, letters, promotional literature, sale flyers, advertisements, newsletters, brochures, slide shows—just about any sales tool you need.

Templates are created in different ways, depending on which software you're using. Templates involve content, design, or both, depending on the desired end product. If that end product is a proposal, the template may involve only content. If it's a slide show, the template will involve a combination of graphics and content.

A template can be as simple as a standard sales letter. You can write the content, save it, and then copy it under a new filename every time you send it to a new prospect. You can replace company names and rewrite passages to customize the letter.

Something to Watch Out For. Be sure to search and replace all company and contact names each time you use a previous letter as a template. Don't miss this step, or you could be in for some embarrassment!

In terms of content, an introductory sales letter should lead with a strong sales "hook." After the hook, describe your offer. Next, give a paragraph about you and your company. Request an appointment.

Tip: Your letters should include a "call-to-action" statement like, "Special pricing is available on Model 201-X if you order before August 15."

Make Your "P.S." Count. According to several studies on how people read a sales letter or direct mail letter, the postscript (P.S.) is usually read first. Use this spot to include your call-to-action statement.

You can create master pages that can contain your letter-head. Also, a master page can be used to customize a letter for your newest prospect or customer. You can insert a name and address, a logo, or other graphics.

In this chapter you will find seven different sales letters to suit common sales situations. Two different proposal formats and a strategic sales plan are provided, too. You can copy and modify all these "templates" to suit your needs. The exercises at the end of this chapter will give you an opportunity to create new letters and proposals—or to enter those you typically use. As you begin to keep templates of all your sales letters, proposals, spread-sheets, working documents, and records, you'll be using your laptop as a "full-service" portable office, the way it is designed to be used.

Search the following list to find a letter or proposal format that may apply to your selling circumstances. You'll also find a list of resources for business letters and some tips for writing and presenting sales proposals as well as for developing a strategic sales plan.

Page	Item

Letter Templates

Letter 1
Introduction 1

[Date]

[Address Block]

Dear _____:

I realize you're very busy, so I'll be brief. We have been asked by other companies in your industry to work closely with their staffs to identify solutions that save time and money and increase productivity.

Frequently, these projects have begun by an initial contact in the [name of person's department]. That's my point in contacting you.

I really would appreciate your help. Can we get together on my next trip to [city] in [month] to discuss the issues you face in controlling costs and increasing production efficiency? At the least, we can brainstorm ideas about where our company may be of value in supporting your efforts.

Thank you for your consideration. I will call you the week of [date] to discuss these ideas and your schedule. I'm confident the short time you invest will be meaningful and productive.

Sincerely,

Your Name
Your Title

Letter 2
Introduction 2

[Date]

[Address Block]

Dear _____:

I am interested in meeting you face-to-face on [date] to get to know you personally and learn about the challenges you face as [position] at [company]. At that time, I would like to introduce you to [your company name]. I am enclosing for your review a brochure that details "who we are and what we're all about."

Our company specializes in _____ _____.

We have completed many programs for [names of customers in prospect's industry] and a host of other organizations that may interest you.

I will call you on [date] to discuss schedules and a time when we can meet.

Sincerely,

Your Company Name Here in Boldface

Your Name
Your Title

Letter 3
Referral (from outside prospect's company)

[Date]

[Address Block]

Dear _____:

I realize you're very busy, so I'll be brief. After speaking with _____ from _____, he (she) recommended I contact you directly.

We've been asked by other companies in your industry to work closely with their staffs to provide products and procedures that save time and money and increase productivity.

I really would appreciate your help. Can we get together on my next trip to [city] in [month] to discuss the issues you face in controlling costs and increasing production efficiency? At the least, we can brainstorm ideas about where our company may be of value in supporting your efforts.

Thank you for your consideration. I will call you the week of [date] to discuss these ideas and your schedule. I'm confident the short time you invest will be meaningful and productive.

Sincerely,

Your Name
Your Title

Letter 4
Referral (from within prospect's company)

[Date]

[Address Block]

Dear _____:

I have spoken with [name within prospect's company], who recommended I contact you directly. After years of working with [company name], [company name], [company name], and others, it's apparent that every sales team faces unique challenges.

Our value is in developing solutions that are business-specific to your people, products, markets, and competitive situation. The enclosed brochure describes our services and closes with a summary of projects that may be of interest.

I would really appreciate your help. Can we meet briefly on [date]? My goal is to explore the most difficult challenges you face regarding [subject].

I will call you the week of [date] to review these ideas and talk about schedules. Thank you for your consideration and a few moments of your time.

Sincerely,

Your Name
Your Title

Enclosure

Letter 5
Confirming Your Appointment

[Date]

[Address Block]

Dear _____:

Thank you for the opportunity to meet with you on [date] at [time]. I am looking forward to reviewing our capabilities and, more importantly, learning the details of your needs and objectives for the coming year. At that time, I hope to offer some creative ideas and recommendations for your consideration.

In summary, we look forward to demonstrating our company's expertise in building customized training solutions for stimulating sales revenue. Thank you, [name] , for your positive consideration and the opportunity to meet with you in [month].

Sincerely,

Your Name
Your Title

Letter 6
"Next Steps" Thank You

[Date]

[Address Block]

Dear _____:

Thank you for meeting with me to discuss the current circumstances at [company]. Our session was important in helping to identify potential areas where we can support your efforts to [insert customer's needs or objectives]

_____

_____

_____.

Based on my notes, I believe our company could be of value in the following areas:

1. _____
   _____

2. _____
   _____

3. _____
   _____

As we discussed, I will take the following actions:

- _____
- _____

Thank you for the opportunity to learn about your position and the structure of the organization. Our goal is to exceed your expectations, no matter what it takes. I look forward to reviewing the results of our efforts during our next meeting at [date].

Sincerely,

Your Name
Your Title

Letter 7
Proposal Thank You

[Date]

[Address Block]

Dear _____:

A brief note of thanks for selecting [your company name] to complete this important project. Everyone in our organization is excited to begin work and deliver the highest-quality services to support you in accomplishing your goals.

In the short time we've spent together, I've grown to appreciate your positive thinking and solution-oriented approach to your job. We are committed to doing whatever it takes to exceed your expectations. Thank you, [name], for your confidence in us.

Sincerely,

Your Name
Your Title

Sources for Business Letters

We have suggested just a handful of business letters you can capture and place on your laptop as templates and adapt as needed. These may or may not work for you. At your local bookstore or through the Web sites of major booksellers and online suppliers, dozens of books are readily available that contain business letters on every topic and for every market. We list just a few of these books below.

Basye, Ann, *Business Letters Ready to Go!* NTC Business Books, 1998, 160 pages, paperback.

Bell, Arthur H., *Complete Business Writer's Manual: Model Letters, Memos, Reports and Presentations for Every Occasion*, Prentice Hall, 1991, 400 pages, hardcover.

Blumenthal, Lassor A., *The Art of Letter Writing: The New Guide to Writing More Effective Letters for All Occasions*, Perigee, 1986, 96 pages, paperback.

Bond, Alan, J., *Over 300 Successful Business Letters for All Occasions*, Barrons, 1998, paperback.

Brusaw, Charles T., Gerald J. Alred, and Walter E. Olin, *The Business Writer's Handbook*, 5th ed., St. Martin's Press, 1997, 691 pages, paperback.

Daniels Booker, Dianna, *Great Personal Letters for Busy People: 300 Ready-to-Use Letters for Every Occasion*, McGraw-Hill, New York, 1997, 384 pages, paperback.

Dugger, Jim, *Business Letters for Busy People*, Career Press, 1995, 256 pages, paperback.

Elliott, Stephen P., *Complete Book Contemporary Business Letters/Strategic Communication*, Round Lake Publishing Company, 1996, 470 pages, paperback.

Geffner, Andrea B., *How to Write Better Business Letters*, 2d ed., Barrons Educational Series, 1995, 144 pages, paperback.

Gorman, Tom, *The Complete Idiot's Almanac of Business Letters and Memos*, Complete Idiot's Guide, 1997, 352 pages, paperback.

Griffin, Jack, *The Complete Handbook of Model Business Letters*, Prentice Hall, 1997, 448 pages, paperback.

Heller, Bernard, *The 100 Most Difficult Business Letters You'll Ever Have to Write, Fax, or E-Mail: Clear Guidance on How to Write Your Way Out of the Toughest Business*, Harperbusiness, New York, 1994, 267 pages, paperback.

Holtz, Herman R., *The Consultant's Guide to Proposal Writing: How to Satisfy Your Client and Double Your Income*, 2d ed., John Wiley & Sons, 1990, 320 pages, hardcover.

Mamchak, Susan P., Steven R. Mamchak, and Lester E. Frailey, *Handbook of Business Letters (Prentice Hall Business Classics)*, 3d ed., Prentice Hall, 1991, 800 pages, paperback.

Merriam-Webster's Guide to Business Correspondence, 2d ed., Merriam-Webster, 1996, 402 pages, hardcover.

Muckian, Michael, with John Woods (contributor), *The Business Letter Handbook: How to Write Effective Letters and Memos for Every Business Situation*, Adams Publishing, 1996, 256 pages, paperback.

Piotrowski, Maryann V., *Effective Business Writing: A Guide for Those Who Write on the Job*, 2d rev. ed., HarperCollins, New York, 1996, 160 pages, paperback.

Poe, Ann, *The McGraw-Hill Handbook of More Business Letters*, McGraw-Hill, New York, 1998, 416 pages, hardcover.

Poe, Roy W., *The McGraw-Hill Handbook of Business Letters*, 3d ed., McGraw-Hill, New York, 1993, 363 pages, paperback.

Porter-Roth, Bud, *Proposal Development: How to Respond and Win the Bid*, 3d ed., Psi Research–Oasis Press, 1998, 250 pages, paperback.

Seglin, Jeffrey L., *The AMA Handbook of Business Letters*, 2d. ed., AMACOM, 1996, hardcover.

Venolia, Jan, *Better Letters: A Handbook of Business and Personal Correspondence*, 2d ed., Ten Speed Press, 1995, paperback.

Werz, Edward W., *Letters That Sell: 90 Ready-to-Use Letters to Help You Sell Your Products, Services and Ideas*, NTC/Contemporary Publishing, 176 pages, paperback.

Tips for Writing Effective Proposals

Take good notes during and right after your sales call. As soon as you leave, immediately review or add to your notes while the meeting is fresh in your mind.

Refer to your meeting notes as you write the proposal, especially your notes about your prospect's needs, desires, concerns, challenges, etc.

Use proposal templates—they can make your sales life a lot easier! Follow these detailed steps:

- Keep standard proposal formats in a master file on your laptop in whatever word processing or basic presentation software you prefer.

- Open your standard proposal format.

- Do an immediate **Save As** using a different filename.

- Recall the new file and make edits or modifications under the new name.

- **Search and Replace** other company names or open fields with the correct prospect name if you are re-saving from a previously created proposal.

- Or follow your software prompts to save a proposal as a template document.

Organize your proposals into logical segments that provide you with natural trial closing opportunities, such as:

- Objectives or Desired End Results
- Current Circumstances
- Overview of Needs
- Recommendations to Meet Needs
- Strategy for Completion/Implementation

- Investment Required
- Summary and Next Steps

Create the objectives, current circumstances, and needs segments of the proposal *based on your knowledge of the customer or prospect.*

In the recommendations section, *use prewritten copy that describes each of the standard components* of your company's offering. Make any necessary edits.

Before the sales call, print a hard copy of your proposal to leave with your prospect. Include a signature and date line on the last page of this version. The prospect can indicate acceptance of the proposal by signing the last page and giving it to you or faxing the signed document back to you.

Develop a separate presentation for testimonials. Have it ready to use during the delivery of a proposal where appropriate. Make it graphical—add color, sound, photos of satisfied customers, even video clips.

On the next few pages, we offer examples of a detailed proposal and an abbreviated proposal.

Proposal Templates

Proposal 1
Detailed Proposal

Your Company Logo Here

Your Company Name

Proposal/Recommendations
for

_____

Project Title and Customer Company Name

Delivered to:

_____

_____

Date

Prepared by

_____

Your Name

Your Company Name
Title of Your Proposal

_____

_____
_____
_____

Dear _____:

Thank you for the opportunity to support you and your team in _____
_____
_____.

These *recommendations* are based on input received from various meetings over the past _____ weeks, including:

_____

_____

_____

_____

_____

_____

I've used a discussion format to present our ideas and suggestions. This format enables us to review our *recommendations* as well as provide opportunities to obtain your input and feedback.

This document has been divided into the following sections:

A.   Project Description
B.   Results
C.   Recommendations
D.   Next-Step Actions
E.   Summary

Your Company Name
Title of Your Proposal

A. Project Description

Based on our past discussions, the *goals/objectives* of our project include:

1. _____
   _____
   _____

2. _____
   _____
   _____

3. _____
   _____
   _____

4. _____
   _____
   _____

5. _____
   _____
   _____

Question: Have we accurately stated your objectives?

Your Company Name
Title of Your Proposal

In order to develop our *recommendations*, we have completed the following *process of work*:

[Identify actions taken to date]

Step 1 _____
_____
_____

Step 2 _____
_____
_____

Step 3 _____
_____
_____

Step 4 _____
_____
_____

Step 5 _____
_____
_____

Step 6 _____
_____
_____

Step 7 The final step in the process included:

- Analyzing all the input received
- Developing our *recommendations*
- Creating this *proposal* for your review and approval

Your Company Name
Title of Your Proposal

B. Results

Based on the project *objectives* and steps completed, we have identified the following *results* for your review.

[Identify initial conclusions or results of your actions taken so far.]

1. _____
_____
_____

2. _____
_____
_____

3. _____
_____
_____

4. _____
_____
_____

5. _____
_____
_____

6. _____
_____
_____

Question: Do the *results* make sense, and are they accurate? Are there any other key findings that we need to consider that will impact achieving our *objectives*?

Your Company Name
Title of Your Proposal

C. Recommendations

Based on input received, we offer the following *recommendations*:

1. _____
   _____
   _____

2. _____
   _____
   _____

3. _____
   _____
   _____

4. _____
   _____
   _____

5. _____
   _____
   _____

Question: Do the *recommendations* make sense and meet the needs of your organization?

Your Company Name
Title of Your Proposal

Investment Required

- _____ . . . . $_____
- _____ . . . . $_____
- _____ . . . . $_____
- _____ . . . . $_____
- _____ . . . . $_____
- _____ . . . . $_____
- _____ . . . . $_____
- _____ . . . . $_____
- _____ . . . . $_____
- _____ . . . . $_____

Total Investment $_____

Payment Terms

Your Company Name
Title of Your Proposal

D. Next-Step Actions

In this section, we have identified a series of *next-step actions* that will move us forward in achieving your objectives.

	Actions	**Target Dates**
1.	_____	_____
2.	_____	_____
3.	_____	_____
4.	_____	_____
5.	_____	_____
6.	_____	_____
7.	_____	_____
8.	_____	_____
9.	_____	_____
10.	_____	_____

Question: Have we identified the appropriate *next-step actions*?

Your Company Name
Title of Your Proposal

E. Summary

Thank you, [name], for the opportunity to work closely with you in completing this important assignment. All of us in [your company name/department] appreciate your confidence and open-minded approach to discussing the key issues and reviewing our recommendations.

Today, we've identified and confirmed the *results*, our *recommendations*, and a *next-step plan* that will guide our actions to help you achieve your *objectives*.

As we discussed early in our relationship, our goal is to:

- Continue to build on the strength of our relationship
- Demonstrate our commitment to you and [customer's company] by providing value-added services and quality products that meet your needs

In summary, let's take the next steps together! Everyone on our team is excited to support you and your team in building sustainable growth and profitability for [customer's company] in the months ahead.

Sincerely,

Your Name
Your Title

Proposal 2
Abbreviated Proposal

Recommendations and Next Steps
Your Company Name

To:_____   From:_____

Subject:_____   Date:_____

Activity

Over the past _____ weeks we have completed a variety of activities to

_____

_____

_____.

To date we have:
[Insert actions taken so far.]

- _____
- _____
- _____
- _____

Results

The results of this activity are summarized below:

- _____
  _____
- _____
  _____
- _____
  _____
- _____
  _____
- _____
  _____
- _____
  _____

Recommendations and Next Steps
Your Company Name

Recommendations

A. _____
   _____
   _____

B. _____
   _____
   _____

C. _____
   _____
   _____

D. _____
   _____
   _____

E. _____
   _____
   _____

F. _____
   _____
   _____

G. _____
   _____
   _____

H. _____
   _____
   _____

I. _____
   _____
   _____

Recommendations and Next Steps
Your Company Name

Investment Required

- _____ . . . . $_____
- _____ . . . . $_____
- _____ . . . . $_____
- _____ . . . . $_____
- _____ . . . . $_____
- _____ . . . . $_____

Total Investment $_____

Next Steps

Actions	Target Dates
1. _____	_____
2. _____	_____
3. _____	_____
4. _____	_____
5. _____	_____
6. _____	_____
7. _____	_____

Thank you, _____, for the opportunity to support your efforts in
_____. Let's take the next steps together for
implementing these *recommendations*. We look forward to providing continued support and value-added services to you and your team in the days
ahead.

Sincerely,

Your Name
Your Title

Tips for Presenting Proposals

During this critical step of the sales process, you are trying to showcase your understanding of a prospect's unique problems while creating confidence in your company's solutions. As you present your proposal, you also want to stimulate interest and tie in every solution or recommendation to your prospect's needs. By your tone of voice and careful qualification questioning, you can assure that your prospect's dominant buying motives are constantly addressed.

During the proposal-delivery process, you're setting the stage for a decision to buy and motivating the prospect to act now. It's a good idea to display confidence, communicate a sense of purpose, continually give assurance, think quickly, and use benefit language and showmanship.

Here are some additional quick tips for success as you present proposals using your laptop:

Add to the proposal content in your own words. Don't just read screens to your prospects. Interpret the main thought on each screen, explain the importance, and communicate why the recommendations are meaningful.

Encourage your prospect to stay involved as you review your statements of objectives, circumstances, and needs. Your opportunities for smaller trial closes will help you close the real sale.

Use trial closing questions in proposals at the end of each segment. For example:

- "Have your *objectives* been stated accurately?"
- "Are the *circumstances* accurate and complete?"
- "Are these *recommendations* on target and do they make sense as a logical path forward?"
- "Whom would you like to lead this project from within your organization?"

Pause as you ask each trial closing question to listen to your customers' comments.

Ask additional questions about any element that requires further clarification.

Get excited, be animated, show enthusiasm and confidence in your recommendations. Be enthusiastic about the importance of moving forward in solving the prospect's problems.

Show client testimonials when appropriate. You might say, "Let me show you what we did for a client who has needs very similar to yours." Briefly explain the circumstances of that project. Then show a testimonial from that satisfied client.

Always be conscious of the time and be prepared to drive the meeting to conclusion without wasting time on less important or irrelevant discussion.

Fully explain your recommendations using clear, concise language. Help the prospect visualize the solution by painting a picture with words. Talk about the implementation phase and ask for agreement with your ideas.

Prepare variations of your recommendations that would be less costly. Just in case your pricing is beyond your prospect's current budget, be able to present other options.

If you see or receive buy-in from the prospect as you present your recommendations, continue to move forward so the prospect can make a buying decision.

Use an "assumed close" if you're already getting buy-in during the presentation. You might say:

- "We are totally prepared to begin work on this important assignment. Let's identify some tentative dates for completing Phase 1."

Or:

- "Based on your feedback, you seem eager to move forward. Let's talk about the key people you feel should be included in the implementation phase."

After delivering the proposal, write a follow-up letter confirming the meeting results and your next-step actions.

Organizing a Strategic Sales Plan

Your laptop computer is a great place to develop and save plans that will help you sell to new prospects and customers in your territory. Here is a "template" you can use to organize your strategic sales plan. Adapt it to your business and use it to track your sales activity, record important customer information, identify sales goals and obstacles, and set target dates for "next steps."

Strategic Sales Plan

Sales Rep _____   Date _____

Company Name _____   Dept./Div. _____

A. Actions completed (to date)

1. _____

2. _____

3. _____

4. _____

5. _____

6. _____

7. _____

8. _____

9. _____

10. _____

B. Identify the customer's greatest needs, challenges, or problem areas.

Department   Needs/Challenges/Problems

_____   _____
                              _____

_____   _____
                              _____

_____   _____
                              _____

_____   _____
                              _____

C. Based on input received, list all the opportunities where you can offer solutions (or added value) to the customer.

_____

_____

_____

_____

_____

_____

_____

_____

D. Overall, what are your objectives? (What do you want to accomplish?)

_____

_____

_____

_____

_____

E. Ultimately, who will make the decision (and impact the decisions) to implement your recommendations?

Department	Decision Maker(s)	Decision Influencer(s)
_____	_____	_____
_____	_____	_____
_____	_____	_____
_____	_____	_____
_____	_____	_____

F. Identify any "red flags" or obstacles that may impact achieving your objectives.

_____

_____

_____

_____

_____

_____

G. Below, identify the elements of your sales plan.

1. What must you do in order to achieve your objectives?

_____

_____

_____

_____

2. How are you going to do it?

                                                                 Target Date

Step 1 _____   _____

Step 2 _____   _____

Step 3 _____   _____

Step 4 _____   _____

Step 5 _____   _____

Step 6 _____   _____

Step 7 _____   _____

3. What resources or support do you need?

_____

_____

_____

_____

_____

Summary

In this chapter, you have looked at a few letter templates that may be appropriate for your selling circumstances, and you have seen a list of resources for locating other excellent business letters.

This chapter has provided some good tips for writing effective proposals and has presented both a long and short proposal format. Plus it has offered some "best practice" tips for presenting proposals using your laptop. In addition, the chapter has provided a template for a strategic sales plan to use as you devise your sales strategy for an existing customer or new prospect.

The exercises at the end of this chapter afford you the opportunity to finish setting up your laptop as a working portable office, complete with sales presentations, frequently used letters, proposal templates, and a strategic sales plan.

How to Avoid the Pitfalls in Writing Letters and Proposals

Pitfall	Try This
It's difficult to find time to write a thank-you letter after an initial call.	• Write one standard thank-you letter template, call it up, do a **Save As** under a new filename, and then customize a few appropriate spots in the letter. • Send it via e-mail, or fax it.
My sales letters tend to be two or three pages long.	• Make it your rule to keep sales letters to one page. Stick to a quick restatement of action taken so far. Then focus on next steps. • Write your letter and let it sit for at least an hour. Go back, reread it, and see what you can cut out. You'll be surprised how a fresh set of eyes will quickly see places to edit and refine. • As you reread your letter, look for places where one word can take the place of three or four words.
Sometimes I get bogged down in the details of the proposal.	• Insert qualifying questions or feedback questions at natural intervals throughout the proposal. • As you present the proposal, summarize key sections rather than reading the detail from every screen. • Use trial closing questions at the end of each segment. • Create a summary section at the end of the proposal. Jump there if you sense your prospect is becoming impatient of the details.
When I have a lot of calls to make or I'm on a sales trip, I have trouble remembering the details about "next steps" I have promised to take with each customer.	• Take a few moments in your car right after a call to make notes on your laptop about the meeting. Or do this in the waiting area, lobby, taxi, or airport gate area. • Use your contact management program on the laptop to write a few details that will jog your memory. • Use the time on the airplane to update the details of each customer you called on during your trip.

Practical Exercises

Exercise 10-1. Adapt one of the seven letter templates in this chapter to your own circumstances. Use the word processing software on your laptop to type in the letter. Or simply copy it, make your edits, and have an assistant enter it into your system.

Exercise 10-2. Do you use standard letters frequently? Are these entered into your laptop? If not, take a few minutes to create these in your word processing program.

Exercise 10-3. Following the abbreviated proposal format shown in this chapter, create a basic PowerPoint presentation you can use to deliver your proposal to a prospect.

Exercise 10-4. Adapt your own proposal letter or document as a simple PowerPoint presentation.

Exercise 10-5. Create a folder on your **C-drive** to hold your strategic plans. Use the sample plan in this chapter to record your activities and identify realistic sales goals for a new target prospect in your territory. How much of the information can you complete today? What information will take some research to complete? Whom will you have to contact to find out about key decision makers? What is your schedule for a path forward?

CHAPTER 11

Traveling with Your Laptop

The fact is, if you're going to sell with your laptop, you'll have to take it with you on the sales call—whether that call is just down the hall to another office, in another city, or halfway across the world. As a result, you'll need to be familiar with some common-sense tips that will help you become more comfortable toting your system, setting it up, hooking it to a projection system, and keeping it in good working order. This chapter gives you some general tips about traveling, hooking up to projection systems, and maintaining your laptop—both physically and in terms of keeping your files backed up, your **Desktop** screen cleaned off, and your operating system free from viruses.

Traveling with Your Laptop

Your Laptop Stays with You. It may seem extremely obvious, but do not check your laptop computer; carry it on the plane with you. Too many salespeople have made this costly mistake. A laptop in its carry case is rugged enough to withstand some turbulence if it's with you inside the passenger cabin, but it won't make it in the cargo hold without damage!

Projectors Can Be Checked. If you have a hard-sided travel case with foam insulation for your projection system, it's OK to check the projector as a piece of luggage.

Make Sure You Can Handle the Projector's Weight. Projection systems range from about 10 pounds to more than 40 pounds. A hard-sided travel case can add 25 pounds of additional weight, and it's very bulky. It's too big for the overhead bins on an airplane and therefore must be checked. The good news is that projectors are becoming smaller, lighter, and less expensive than their bulky predecessors, but they're equally functional.

Your Laptop Always Goes on Top of Other Items. The display screen is extremely vulnerable to damage. Even a little weight on top of your laptop can push the display screen into the keyboard and cause the screen to crack. If it cracks, you're out of luck—when the display screen is damaged, the image essentially shatters. You won't be able to see anything clearly enough to work with the machine.

Tip: When you're stacking all your rolling carrying luggage for the trek down the airport concourse, put your laptop case on top of the stack. Or arrange your bags so that nothing heavy is resting on top of your laptop carrying case.

Treat Your Laptop Gently. Take care opening and *especially closing* the lid. If you close the lid too forcefully, you can damage the fastening mechanism or even crack the display screen.

Accessories

Laptop accessories are items you need in order to streamline the use of your laptop, particularly when traveling. You won't want to overlook these in making your purchasing decisions.

Carrying Cases. From fancy leather cases to vinyl to canvas, laptop carrying cases come in all styles and sizes. And they don't come with the laptop. They're extra—you have to buy one.

When you go to purchase one, consider the weight and strength of your carrying case. Hard-sided or leather cases are very strong, but they're heavy. It may be better to get a soft-sided case of lightweight material. Cases made of synthetic fabrics and padding (cordura, nylon, etc.) are very strong and light.

Although laptops are becoming more lightweight with every new generation, on average they still weigh between 9 and 11 pounds. For salespeople not used to taking a laptop on the road, these extra pounds can make a difference in the hassle at the airport and in rushing to the next appointment. You might want to try a combination briefcase and laptop carrying case that comes on rollers and has an extension handle. That way you'll be pulling the weight more often than lifting it.

Surge Protectors. A surge protector prevents your computer from being affected by fluctuations in the electrical power supply. Computer components are delicate and can be severely damaged in a millisecond by an unexpected surge in power. Some surge protectors also allow you to plug in other equipment.

Power Strips. A power strip may look like a surge protector, but it's not. It's a rectangular box with up to six three-pronged outlets in it. The strip plugs into the wall or your three-pronged extension cord on one end. You can plug your laptop and up to five other devices into one strip.

When you're on the road with your projection system, carry a power strip. You'll probably have three devices (projector, laptop, and VCR) to plug in right off the bat, and possibly more. Hotels don't usually provide power strips. Extension cords, yes. Power strips, no.

Extension Cords. Carry at least one extension cord with you whenever you travel with your laptop and/or projection system. Attach a single-plug surge protector to the end of your extension cord.

Safety Precaution: Tape all power cords to the floor with duct tape to prevent tripping.

Tip: After you turn off your computer or projector, unplug the power cord from the power strip first—before you remove it from the computer or projector power port.

Phone Cords. Carry at least one telephone cord in your laptop case. It may come in handy when you're ready to fax a document or retrieve your e-mail.

Extra Batteries. Carry one extra set of batteries for each device that requires them. Make sure that they're fresh and they're the right size.

Portable Printers. One option for *shoulder-to-shoulder* salespeople is to invest in one of the tiny printers now available on the market. Take it with you on the road. You can print your documents at the hotel, in the lobby, or during your sales call. They're small enough to fit easily into your carrying case, and they weigh almost nothing!

Hookup Tips

If you purchase a projection system, it's smart to work with the system first before taking it with you on the road. Read the setup manual first before you unpack the new projector. Use a highlighter pen to highlight important sections of the manual so you can find them easily later.

Next, read it again, and unpack each item as you go through the manual the second time. Item by item, place everything out on a large surface and make a list of what's there.

Packing List. If you travel with your laptop and a multimedia projector, try creating a personal packing list you can double-check to make sure you have everything you need with you. Your list might look something like this:

Sample Packing List

✓ Laptop computer	✓ Remote control cable
✓ Computer case	✓ Remote mouse
✓ Power cord for laptop	✓ Cables and jacks to connect laptop to projector audio/video equipment
✓ Laptop user's manual	
✓ Projector	✓ Necessary adapters
✓ Projector user's manual	✓ Extra batteries
✓ Power cord for projector	✓ Interchangeable CD-ROM drive and disk drive
✓ Lens cap	
✓ Projector remote control and batteries	✓ CD-ROM and presentation disks
	✓ Telephone cable
	✓ Other items

Label All Connection Cords. Several cords will come with your projection system. Try tagging every cord separately with its correct name, using self-adhesive labels. The name should match the name in the user's manual. Tag all connector ports with their correct names in the same way. Or use a color-coding system if that works better for you. For example, the green-tagged connector goes in the green-tagged port.

The newer laptops and projection systems label their cords and connectors with words and/or icons that you can easily match up.

Prep and Setup. Allow a minimum of 45 to 50 minutes to set up your equipment before the meeting. If possible, set up and test your equipment in the meeting room the night before your presentation and make sure the room will be locked. Depending on the size of your meeting room, we suggest that you place the projector no more than 10 to 20 feet away from the screen so that the projected image is not too large.

Set the projector to **Standby** when you come to any kind of a break. Arrive back from the break 5 minutes early to reactivate the projector and give it time to warm up. It will return you to the same spot where you left off.

Tip: If you do not have access to your presentation room beforehand to set up, you can set up the equipment, connect all the cables, and test the system in your hotel room. Call a porter for a cart, and place all your equipment (already set up and connected) onto the cart. Roll the cart to your meeting room and transfer the equipment to the projection table. Plug in the power strip to the wall socket, hook up to the meeting room VCR, and you're ready to go!

Starting the Laptop and Projector. When your laptop and projection system are connected, follow your user's manual for instructions on how to turn on the system.

Switch on Laptop Last. With some computers, the order in which you power up the equipment is very important. It is recommended that you always turn on the computer *last*. Turn on all other pieces of equipment before you turn on the computer.

Once your projection system and laptop are on, you may not be able to see an image on your computer screen. On most models, you will be able to view the image on the projector and laptop screens simultaneously. Some older models, however, will only let you view the image on one screen or the other, not both.

Shutting Down the Laptop and Projector. Close your presentation, turn the projector off, and shut down the laptop—and in that order.

- *To shut down the projector,* simply turn its **Power** switch off. Disassemble the individual pieces and cables. Replace them in your projector case just the way you extracted them so you can access them easily for your next presentation.

- *To shut down the computer,* point to the **Start** button and choose **Shut Down.** The computer will prompt you with a window and a question, "Shut down the computer?" Click **Yes** if you are ready to completely shut down the laptop. The computer will shut itself down, and the projector will project a plain field.

Note: When you disconnect the projector after you have switched it off, always remove the power cord from the electrical outlet first. Then remove it from the projector.

Care and Maintenance

Your laptop needs very little maintenance. Follow these tips for general care:

Use Electricity at the Office. Keep the laptop plugged in at home or the office. No need to waste battery power.

Keep Batteries Charged. On the road, plug your laptop in overnight to keep the batteries pumped up.

Point with Your Finger. Avoid using a pen or pencil to point to the display screen. These marks are very hard to remove.

Clean the Screen. Clean your display screen once in awhile, especially if you use the *shoulder-to-shoulder* technique of pointing to the screen with your finger during your sales presentations.

Spray the Cloth, Not the Screen. Power down and unplug your system before you clean it. Use an antistatic cleaning solution, but don't spray the screen directly. Spray the solution onto a soft, clean cloth and then wipe the display screen. You can also buy pretreated cleaning cloths specifically designed for cleaning computers. 3M, among other companies, manufactures these pretreated cloths. Check with your local computer store.

Clean the Keyboard. Use the same method as above to clean the keyboard and remove the dirt and grease that builds up. Make sure the system is off first. Remember to spray the cloth instead of the keyboard. Avoid spraying any cleaning solution into the keyboard because moisture will damage the components. Don't dig the lint out with anything sharp or try to shake the machine to dislodge debris.

Vacuum Once in a While. Most manufacturers recommend using a hand-held vacuum with a special attachment to remove the dust and lint that collect between the keys on your keyboard or in the vents of the casing. Or you can use canned air spray to blow the dust out. You probably won't have to do this very often unless you work in a dusty environment.

Clean Your Pointing Devices. Clean your trackball, touchpad, or joystick pointer with a damp cloth or cotton swab. Make sure the laptop is off and unplugged first.

Clean the Mouse. If you use a mouse, you'll notice that after a while it may not be as sensitive as it used to be. Remove the cord from your laptop. Turn the mouse over, take the plate off, remove the ball, and shake/blow the dust and lint out of the cavity. Clean the ball with a damp cloth and then put it back.

    Tip: Keep your coffee cup and any beverages well away from the laptop. If you spill drinks into your keyboard, you'll be purchasing a new system.

Batteries and Power Management

When you travel with your laptop, you'll need to watch how much battery power your laptop is using. Laptops run on electricity or battery power. We're not talking about the AAA batteries you get at the grocery store. Laptop batteries are larger than that. They're rechargeable and come in three types:

- NiCad (nickel-cadmium batteries)—old style
- NiMH (nickel-metal-hydride)—better
- Lithium-ion—best

Take an extra set of recharged batteries or a freshly charged battery pack with you on the road if you're doing a lot of work on the plane. Check how much battery power you have left. Your laptop owner's manual will explain how to recharge and manage the battery system.

Your system has settings you can choose to conserve battery power. These settings also allows you to set automatic **Sleep**, **Suspend** or **Hibernation** periods. To get the most out of your batteries, set your system to automatically **Suspend** after so many minutes of inactivity. When you need to deliver a lengthy presentation (over an hour), plug your laptop into the wall whenever possible to ensure adequate power.

If you use a remote mouse for the laptop and or remote control for your projector, be sure to carry a full set of spare batteries for each device.

Laptop Battery Disposal. Consult your user's manual for how to properly dispose of or recycle the batteries from your system. In many states, the chemicals used to power your batteries are regulated.

Backing Up Your Work

Save Your Work First. On the road or at the home office, make it a habit to save your work often. The definition of "often" depends on you. Save every time you close a file (the system forces you to save). Save every 15 to 30 minutes if the file you're working on is open for several hours. Or set your software programs to save at preset intervals. In the airplane, you'll want to save your work frequently.

Save More Often on Battery Power. Be careful to save your work when you're on battery power. You could lose half of that important report or proposal in the blink of an eye! When the battery is about to go out, the system will usually prompt you to save your work.

Back Up Your Work Every Day. Hard drives don't last forever, and some of them crash and die unexpectedly for a variety of reasons. If you're relying on your laptop hard drive to store all your files, you could be in for a nasty surprise.

What to Back Up. Back up whatever files you have worked on today—contact management files, letters, memos, proposals, presentations, e-mails you have sent or received, any files downloaded from e-mail, etc.

How to Back Up. Windows 98 and Windows NT systems have an automatic backup program that will prompt you to copy the contents of your hard drive onto some kind of external backup media like a floppy disk, a tape backup, or an Iomega Zip™ drive (Zip disks hold 100 Mbytes) or Jaz™ drive (Jaz cartridges hold 1000 Mbytes).

- In the case of a tape backup device or a Zip or Jaz drive, you would connect your laptop to the device via the appropriate cable (you must also have the accompanying software loaded on your system so your laptop will recognize the backup device).

- Create a new backup folder on your backup tape, diskette, or cartridge. Label it "Backup." Click and drag the current files from your laptop onto the new folder.

Back Up on the Road. Take floppy diskettes with you on the road—always carry two or three blank floppies. Insert them into the floppy drive on your laptop to click and drag your current work to the diskette.

Label Your Backup Floppies. You may end up with a stack of backup floppy diskettes. Take the time every day to label them so you'll know what's on each of them. Otherwise, you may have to insert and look through dozens of unlabeled or incorrectly labeled floppies to find what you need.

Organizing Your Desktop and Keeping It "Clean"

In Chapter 1, "Preparing for the Call," you learned to make a **Shortcut** for your presentations and other documents. The **Shortcut** icon will appear on the **Desktop** screen. You can double-click the icon to launch the software and open your file.

Organizing your presentations is simple. Make **Shortcuts** for all your frequently used presentations, price sheets, charts, worksheets, etc.—everything you refer to in a sales call. As the icons appear on your **Desktop** screen, click on each icon once to select it, and then drag it to a place on the screen where you can easily find it. Put similar presentation icons together in the same area of your screen.

Use Your Desktop Like a Real Desk. That's why it's called the **"Desktop."** Your current work at the office is probably organized in folders—or at least in stacks of papers—that sit on top of your desk so you can find them quickly. The **Desktop** on your computer acts the same way. Keep the current files and frequently used presentations there. If too many items accumulate, create a new folder on your hard drive and drop the items in there. They'll still be easy to find.

Protect against Viruses. Be aware that all computers—including your laptop—are vulnerable to computer viruses, which can damage your files and operating system, causing the system to behave erratically, or even destroying your hard drive and every file on it. A virus is like a self-replicating parasite written on purpose to change how your computer behaves. All of this can happen without your knowledge or permission.

Contracting a Virus. Your laptop can get a virus when you share disks between computers, through e-mail, or by downloading material from your company's Intranet or the Internet.

Getting Rid of a Virus. Most newer systems will have a software utility already loaded on them, like Norton Anti-Virus. The software automatically checks for viruses—or chunks of data that seem to act like viruses—and alerts you to their presence. You can run the software program to delete the virus and repair any damaged files.

Tip: If your system does not contain antivirus software, be sure to purchase a package at your local computer store. As a registered owner, you can receive updates of new virus definitions (a file containing the antivirus programs) to keep your system protected against any new viruses. Unfortunately, new viruses are discovered every day.

Tip: Copy your clean system folder and keep the copy in a safe place. You'll have it in the event that you need to completely restore it as a result of a virus infection.

Summary

Your laptop can enhance your sales process when you're traveling. And it doesn't have to be a hassle to take it with you—not if you use the commonsense tips in this chapter.

Soon, you will come to rely on your laptop as a full-service portable office, and you won't want to be without it whether you're at home or on a sales trip. With your **Desktop** well organized and your sales support materials easily accessible—everything you need for a sales call at your fingertips—you're ready for *Shoulder-to-Shoulder Selling*.

How to Avoid the Pitfalls When You Travel with Your Laptop

Pitfall	*Try This*
My laptop is too heavy and awkward to lug on the plane.	• Use a rolling briefcase with a compartment for your laptop. Store the briefcase under the seat rather than in the overhead bin. Your lifting will be confined to taking the case in and out of the car and lifting it onto the security X-ray platform at the airport. • Check carefully for weight next time you or your MIS department purchases a new computer. The newer models are lighter than ever before.
My laptop was damaged in the airport during my last trip.	• Avoid putting any other piece of luggage on top of your laptop carrying case. Roll it by itself (if you have a roller model), or place it on top of your stack of other luggage. • Don't check your laptop like luggage. Keep the system with you in the passenger cabin.
The conference room did not have enough outlets.	• Carry a power strip and surge protector with you. • Always carry an extension cord.
My batteries run out often when I travel.	• Take an extra set of charged batteries with you. • Set your system to **Suspend** after 10 to 15 minutes of inactivity to conserve battery power. • Plug in your laptop wherever possible. • Plug your laptop (system off) into the wall outlet overnight to recharge the batteries. • Check your user's manual. Some models must fully discharge their batteries before they will take a full charge again. • Take extra sets of the correct batteries for your projector remote, laser pointer, and remote mouse.
I thought I had saved my latest proposal, but it's lost.	• Save your work often (minimum of once an hour), or set your system to automatically back up every 15 or 30 minutes. • Back up current files daily, whether you're at the office or on a sales trip.
I never seem to have enough time to set up the projector before my meeting.	• Allow a minimum of 45 to 50 minutes for the setup and testing process.

Practical Exercises

Exercise 11-1. Using the list on page 182 as a model, create your own packing list for traveling. Print it and place it in your laptop carrying case for future reference.

Exercise 11-2. If you or your company owns a projection system that travels with you, take a moment to label all connection cords as described in this chapter.

Exercise 11-3. Locate the power management and battery discussion in your hardware user's manual. Take the system battery out and examine it. Read the manual to discover whether your battery must be completely discharged before it can take a full charge again. Take the time to understand your battery setup and operation. Determine how to check the battery level on your system. Is there an indicator on the keyboard, or do you check on the screen?

Exercise 11-4. Check your display screen for smudges or fingerprints. Use the correct method, as described in the chapter, to clean the screen.

A Final Word

"Don't look back—someone might be gaining on you," the great baseball player Satchel Paige once said. He was right. And when it comes to selling, Paige's words are right on the money. You can't afford to look back, not with the speed at which business and commerce are conducted today across the globe. Your competitors are gaining on you, and you'll need every advantage to stay ahead of them. As you draw upon your sales experience to solve the challenges and issues for customers and prospects, your enhanced ability to communicate through a laptop computer will serve you well.

It's common knowledge that the profession we call "selling" is the linchpin of all commerce and industry. Nothing happens until somebody sells something. The skill sets you use to present sales information with your laptop will quickly become the fundamentals of your craft—the basics, if you will, that through constant, consistent application you will claim as professional habits in your day-to-day selling. These skills will separate you from your peers, differentiate you from the competition, and put you on top!

As you know, the sales call itself is a key element in the race against your competition. In our 25 years in the sales training industry, we believe that competence is *the* career difference in this race for any salesperson. Competence represents a combination of your knowledge and the successful application of your professional skills. Also, as you have learned in *How to Sell with a Laptop*, preparation is critical to the development of your competence, confidence, and credibility as a professional. Now that you have the tools, you're ready to prepare for your next sales call.

As you have discovered, the use of your laptop can and will touch every aspect of your daily sales activity—from prospecting and account management to communication, presentation, and follow-up. Because our world is moving "at the speed of business"—a new, faster-than-ever-before speed at which salespeople must now travel—you need to be comfortable with the tool that will help you reach top speed and stay well ahead of the field.

Thanks for letting us share with you several ways to improve your position in this high-speed race called selling. In completing *How to Sell with a Laptop*, you have taken a major step toward the future of your selling career—and you'll never look back again!

Good selling!

Laptop 101 for New Users

1. How to Start Your Laptop

See your laptop user's manual and study the diagrams that show the components of the laptop machine itself. Next, using those diagrams, locate the **Power** switch and push it or slide it to the "on" position. The system will begin to "boot," which means it will initialize and load the resident software programs it needs to operate properly.

2. Your Windows *Desktop* Screen

The **Desktop** is the main screen your laptop shows once the system has booted. It's called the **Desktop** because it's supposed to act just like your desktop at the office. Your current paperwork piles up in folders and stacks. It's the same metaphor on your laptop screen (Figure A-1).

On your **Desktop** screen you'll see a background field, some icons, and a **Taskbar**.

Figure A-1. Your laptop **Desktop** screen.

The **Desktop** screens are virtually the same for Windows 95, Windows 98, and Windows NT. Each shows at least these five main icons, as follows:

- **My Computer**
- **Recycle Bin**
- **Inbox**
- **Internet Explorer**
- **My Briefcase**

My Computer. Double-click this icon, usually in the upper left corner of your **Desktop** screen, to open it. It's an easy way to see what's on your computer and browse through the folders and files (Figure A-2).

Recycle Bin. Drag files you no longer want to keep to the **Recycle Bin**. When you're sure you want to get rid of them, double-click on the **Recycle Bin** icon. From the **File** menu, click **Empty Recycle Bin** (Figure A-3).

Inbox. The **Inbox** is the icon for Microsoft Exchange, the embedded program through which you can send and receive e-mail or fax messages. You can double-click the **Inbox** icon to open Microsoft Exchange to send or receive your messages (Figure A-4).

Internet Explorer. This is the built-in Microsoft Internet Web browser (Figure A-5).

Figure A-2. My Computer icon.

Figure A-3. Recycle Bin icon.

My Briefcase. If you work on a desk model computer at the office, but use your portable laptop at home and on the road, you can use **My Briefcase** as an aid to keep the documents on your office desk model current. Provided the two computers are cabled together or plugged into the same network, you can drag files from the shared folders on your desk model to the **My Briefcase** icon on your laptop. Once you've worked on the files at home or away, you can use **My Briefcase** to automatically update the older files on your office desk model with the most current ones (Figure A-6).

Taskbar. The **Taskbar** usually appears across the bottom of the **Desktop** screen (although you can customize its location). It serves as an easy way to find a file, get help, start a program, or shut down the system. The names of active applications appear on the **Taskbar.** You can use these buttons to quickly switch between applications. In addition, a clock can be found in a special tool area on the right side of the **Taskbar.** Other tools may be found there—specific to your computer (Figure A-7).

Start Button. This is the main function button on the **Taskbar.** Use it to start a program or find a file. It's also the quickest way to get to help (Figure A-8).

Figure A-4. Inbox icon.

Figure A-5. Internet Explorer icon.

Figure A-6. My Briefcase icon.

Windows Explorer. Another good thing to know about your **Desktop** is **Windows Explorer**. From here you can view the hierarchy of all the folders and files on your computer. Use it to move files from one folder to another or to copy files. To find **Windows Explorer,** go to the **Taskbar,** click the **Start** button, and point to **Programs**. A long list of programs appears. Find **Windows Explorer** and click on it (Figure A-9).

Figure A-7. Windows **Taskbar**.

Figure A-8. Start button, usually appearing in the left corner of the **Taskbar**

Figure A-9. The **Windows Explorer** window shows the folders and files on your system.

3. Setting the System to *Suspend*

Consult your laptop user's manual first. For a Windows 95 laptop, click the **Start** button on the **Taskbar** and choose **Suspend**.

Setting the System to *Suspend*	
Windows 98 Instructions	*Windows NT Instructions*
From the **Start** button select **Shut Down** and then click **Standby**. Consult your hardware user's manual for how to wake up the system.	Windows NT does *not* offer a **Suspend** option from the **Start** button. You can only **Shut Down** and then confirm in the dialog box whether you really want to **Shut Down** or **Restart**. Consult your hardware user's manual for specifics on how to **Suspend** and wake up your system.

4. "Waking Up" the System

Each laptop is a little different, so check your user's guide for details. Sometimes you can wake your system by pressing any key or by pressing the on/off switch.

5. Installing and Running Software

First Way to Install and Run Software (Windows 95). If the new software comes on diskettes, insert the first program disk into the floppy disk drive (**A-drive**). If you're installing software from a CD-ROM disk, insert it into the CD-ROM drive (**D-drive**).

From the **Start** button, point to **Settings** and select **Control Panel**. The **Control Panel** will display a window containing several icons. Find the icon called **Add/Remove Programs** and double-click it (Figure A-10).

Figure A-10. You can install software by using the **Add/Remove Programs** icon in **Control Panels**. The buttons in the top right corner of the window allow you to **Minimize** the window to the **Taskbar** or **Maximize** it to fill the screen for easy viewing.

Follow the installation instructions in the dialog window. The installer program will ask you to enter the destination drive and directory. Some installer programs give you a default location—usually on the **C-drive** (your hard drive) under **Programs**.

If the installer does not offer a default location, you'll be asked to create a new folder on the hard drive and copy the application's file into that new folder. Here's how to do that:

- Double-click the **My Computer** icon on the **Desktop**.

- Locate the **C-drive** icon in the **My Computer** window. Double-click it to open it.

- From there you can create and label a new folder by clicking on **File** along the top of the window and selecting **New** from the drop-down menu. Choose **Folder**.

- A new folder will appear. Type in a new name for the folder to match your new application—so you can easily find it.

Continuing installation, you'll be prompted when to insert each additional diskette. When installation is complete, read the information in the dialog window for additional instructions. In most cases, you have to restart your system to use the new software.

Second Way to Install and Run Software. Insert the first diskette (in a set of floppies), or insert the application CD-ROM into the appropriate drive on your laptop. Use **My Computer**, double-click on the **A-drive** (diskettes) or **D-drive** (CD-ROM) to find that program's icon, open it, and view the contents. A window pops up showing the contents of the program diskette or CD-ROM. Within the window, find the "setup" or "install" icon and double-click it. Follow the installation instructions.

Installing and Running Software

Note: Windows 95, Windows 98, and Windows NT are identical for installing and running software.

To install a program:

From the **Start** button, point to **Settings** and click on **Control Panels**.

Double-click the **Add/Remove Programs** icon.

Click the **Install** button and follow the instructions. Windows 98 looks for an installation program on your disk drives and installs it.

To run a program:

From the **Start** button, point to **Programs**, select the name of the program you want, and click on it once.

6. Adding a Program to the *Start* Button

Open **My Computer**. Find the folder you've created for your new application program. Click on the program icon and drag it to the **Start** button. When you release the mouse (or pointing device), the program is loaded as an item at the top of the **Start** button. Now you can access the application by simply clicking on **Start**.

7. Making a *Shortcut* on the *Desktop*

On your Windows **Desktop** screen, a **Shortcut** is a symbol that stands for something else, like a real application program or presentation file. You can create **Shortcuts** to make it easier to find the applications and files you use most often. You can even make **Shortcuts** for your disk drives (**A-drive, C-drive, D-drive, or E-drive**) to make them easier to find—plus these new **Shortcuts** will function exactly the same as their icons would within the **My Computer** folder. Follow either of two ways to make a **Shortcut** in Windows 95.

First way. Find the file for which you want a **Shortcut**. Click once on the file to select it, but do not open it. On the **File** menu, click **Create Shortcut**. Next, drag the new **Shortcut** icon to the **Desktop**.

Second way. Open **My Computer** and find the application folder. Click it to open. Use the right button on your mouse, touchpad, or other pointing device to drag the program icon onto your **Desktop**. When you release the right mouse button, you'll see a menu. Choose the **Create Shortcuts Here** option. This creates a **Shortcut** icon to that program. It will then appear on your **Desktop**.

Adding a Program to the *Start* Button	
Windows 95 and Windows 98 Instructions	*Windows NT Instructions*
Open **My Computer** and find the program you want to appear on the **Start** menu.	This step is a bit more involved in Windows NT than in Windows 95 and 98.
Click on it and drag it to the **Start** button.	First, create a folder on your hard drive to receive the new program.
Let go of your mouse or other pointing device.	Copy the program to that folder.
Your program will now appear on the **Start** menu.	Click on the **Start** button, and point to **Settings**.
	Click on **Taskbar**, then on the **Start Menu Programs**.
	Choose the **Add** button and click on **Browser**. Then open the folder into which you have copied the program.
	Double-click on the program icon you want to add.
	Choose **Next** and then double-click on the folder where you want your program to appear on the **Start** menu.
	Enter a name for the program, and click **Finish**. Then click **OK** at the bottom of the dialog box.
	Your program will now appear on the **Start** menu.

Making a *Shortcut* on the *Desktop*
Note: Windows 95, Windows 98, and Windows NT are the same for this function.
Open **My Computer** folder. Use the right mouse button (or touchpad or pointing device) to click on the icon you want and drag it over to the **Desktop**. Release the right mouse button and choose **Create Shortcut Here** from the menu.

8. Finding and Opening an Existing Folder or File

As usual, you have several choices. Try this first. Click on the **Start** button, point to **Find**, and choose **Files or Folders**. A dialog box will appear. Where it says **Named**, type all or part of the file's name. Click **Find Now**. The system will search for a match and display the name and location of any matching files or folders.

To see all files and filename extensions, use **My Computer** or **Windows Explorer**. Either of these will show what's on your laptop.

Click **My Computer** to see a display of folders and files. Double-click any that you want to see. The contents will be displayed.

Or use the **Start** button to find and choose **Windows Explorer**. A window will appear containing folders (on the left) and files (on the right).

To open a folder or file, find it and double-click it.

Finding and Opening an Existing Folder or File	
Windows 95 and Windows 98 Instructions	*Windows NT Instructions*
From the **Start** button, point to **Find** and choose **Files or Folders**.	The Windows 98 steps for finding files, folders, or words within files will work for Windows NT, too.
Type in all or part of the file or folder title in the **Find** program dialog box.	Windows NT gives you an interesting option. You can actually see what's contained in an icon without opening an application program to view its contents.
Or type an unusual word you might remember from the content of the file in the **Containing Text** window.	
Tip: Unusual words will narrow your search more than common words.	• Use the **Quick View** feature by pointing to an icon and clicking the right mouse button. A menu appears.
Click **Find Now** in the dialog box. The system will display any matching folders or files and their location.	• Choose **Quick View** from the menu. Next, you'll see a small window displaying the content of the file.
Go to the folder you've found, double-click to open it, look for the file you want, and double-click on it to open it.	• With **Quick View** you can look through a number of similar looking files without taking the time to load the program in order to see the contents of the file.

9. Creating a New Folder

First decide where you want your new folder to reside. Using **My Computer** or **Windows Explorer**, open the folder in which the new folder will reside. Go to the **File** menu and select **New**. Click **Folder**. The new folder will appear. Type in a new name for the new folder and press **Enter**.

Creating a New Folder

Note: Windows 95, Windows 98, and Windows NT are the same for this function.

From the **Start** button, go to **Programs** and choose **Windows Explorer**.

On the left side of the **Explorer** window, click once on the folder where you want the new folder to live.

The contents of that folder will appear in the right side of the window.

Use your right mouse button to click on the right side of the **Explorer** window. A menu appears.

Point to **New** and choose **Folder**.

Type the name of the new folder and press **Enter**.

---

10. Creating a New File

Whether you're working in Windows 95, Windows 98, or Windows NT, all new files are created from within the application program you're using. For example, if you wanted to create a new letter in Microsoft Word, first open Word and choose **New** from the **File** menu. A new file will appear. Enter your work and then save the file. The same general procedure applies to creating a new PowerPoint presentation, Excel spreadsheet, etc.

11. Saving a File

For Windows 95, Windows 98, and Windows NT operating systems, new and edited files are saved from within the application in which they were created. To save a file, choose **Save** from the

File menu or use the keyboard commands **[Ctrl] + [S]**. Select or create a folder to put the new file in and give the file a name. Click **Save**.

Or from any application program running on either of the three operating systems, press and release the **Alt, F,** and **S** keys: **[Alt] + [F] + [S]**. This will save your work.

Save As. To modify an existing file, but still preserve your original work, use the **Save As** command from the **File** menu. A dialog box will appear. Type in a new name for your modified file, and then click the **Save** button. Now you will have two separate files. The newly created modified file becomes your active window.

Note: Save As acts just like **Save** when you're saving a brand new file.

12. Moving and Copying a File

Traditional Copying. Using **My Computer** or **Windows Explorer**, choose the file or folder you want to copy. From the **Edit** menu, click **Copy**. Open the folder or disk where you want to put the copied folder or file. On the **Edit** menu, click **Paste**.

Drag-and-Drop Moving and Copying. Windows 95 gives you the option to drag folders or files to change their location in your system. Use the left mouse button to drag and move a file. Use the right mouse button to drag and copy a file.

- *To move a file,* you can open the folder that contains the file you're copying, and then use the left mouse button to drag it to the folder you want to move it to.

- *To copy a file,* use the right mouse button to drag it to the folder you want to copy it into.

Copying a File onto a Diskette. With a diskette in the floppy drive, use **My Computer** or **Windows Explorer** to select the **A-drive** and find the file you want to copy. With that file highlighted, go to the **File** menu and choose **Send To**. Then select the floppy disk drive. The file will copy to the disk.

Tip: You can copy more than one file or folder at a time by holding down the **Ctrl** key while you click all the items you want to copy.

Moving and Copying a File

Note: Windows 95, Windows 98, and Windows NT are the same for this function.

To move a file: Click the file you want to move and drag it to its new location.

To copy a file: Hold down **Ctrl**. Then click the file you want to copy and drag it to its new location.

---

13. Printing a File

In Windows 95, if a file is open, you can print it by pointing to the **File** menu and choosing **Print**. Follow the instructions in the dialog window.

If the file is closed, drag its icon from **My Computer** or **Windows Explorer** to your printer in the **Printers** folder. Follow the instructions in the dialog window.

Tip: Make a **Shortcut** on the **Desktop** for your printer to make it easier to find and access. (See item 15 on page 210.)

Printing a File

Note: Windows 95, Windows 98, and Windows NT are the same for this function.

When the file is open, press **Alt** then **F** then **P** in that order [**Alt**] + [**F**] + [**P**].

Or choose **Print** from the **File** pull-down menu.

If the file is not open, drag its icon from **My Computer** or **Windows Explorer** to your printer icon in the **Printers** folder.

14. Closing a File or Folder

In Windows 95, every window has an × (close button) in the upper right corner. Click the × to close an active window, which closes the file or folder. Or while the window is active, choose **Close** from the **File** menu.

If you have not saved your work, a dialog box will appear prompting you to save before you can close the file.

Closing a File or Folder

Note: Windows 95, Windows 98, and Windows NT are the same for this function.

Save your work first with the command **[Ctrl] + [S]**.

Close the file or folder window by clicking the × in the upper right corner.

---

15. Making a Printer *Shortcut* on Your *Desktop*

You can also make a **Shortcut** to your printer on the **Desktop** screen. Start by finding the icon for your printer in the **Printers** folder. Click it and then go to the **File** menu. Choose **Create Shortcut**. Drag the **Shortcut** icon onto the **Desktop**.

Now when you need to print a file, just drag the file icon onto your printer **Shortcut** icon. A dialog window will appear. Follow the instructions in the dialog window, and the file will print.

Making a Printer *Shortcut* on Your *Desktop*

Note: Windows 95, Windows 98, and Windows NT are the same for this function.

Go to the **Printers** folder and use the right mouse button to click on your printer.

From the pop-up menu choose **Create Shortcut**.

Drag the **Shortcut** icon to the **Desktop**.

---

16. Maximizing/Minimizing Active Windows

Any active window has a title bar along the top. Three other buttons appear on the title bar: An × to close the window, a **Maximizer** button, and a **Minimizer** button (Figure A-11).

Click the **Maximizer** button to make the window full screen. Click it again and the window returns to its original size.

The **Minimizer** button keeps the window active but makes it disappear to a button on the **Taskbar**. The button is now labeled with the window title. Click that button and the window reappears.

Maximize or **Minimize** all windows by using your right mouse button. To do this, click a blank area of the **Taskbar**; a pop-up menu appears. Click **Minimize All Windows** from the pop-up menu. All active windows (except for dialog boxes) will appear as small buttons on the **Taskbar**. You can restore them individually by clicking on each button, or you can use your right mouse button to click a blank area on the **Taskbar** and choose **Undo Minimize All** (Figures A-12 and A-13).

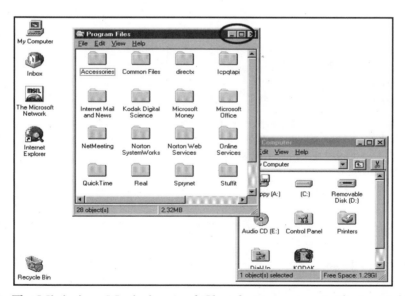

Figure A-11. The **Minimizer, Maximizer,** and **Close** button appear in the top right corner of every working window.

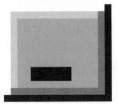

Figure A-12. Minimizer button.

Figure A-13. Maximizer button.

Maximizing/Minimizing Active Windows

Note: Windows 95, Windows 98, and Windows NT are the same for this function.

You'll find three buttons in the upper right corner of every window:

- The **Minimizer** button
- The **Maximizer** button
- The **Restore** button*

Click the **Minimizer** button to make a window disappear and become a button along the **Taskbar**. Click the **Taskbar** button to make the window increase to normal working size.

With a window at normal size, click the **Maximizer** button to make the window expand to take up most of the screen.

*With a window at full size, the **Maximizer** button becomes the **Restore** button. Click it to restore the window to normal working size.

17. Accessing the Internet

To access and use the Internet from your laptop, connect a phone cord from your laptop to a phone jack in the wall. Some hotels now provide a dedicated data jack connection for computer communications access.

If your laptop modem resides on a PC card, make sure the card is in the proper slot.

Double-click on the program icon for your Web browser (Windows Internet Explorer, America Online, Netscape Navigator, CompuServe, AT&T, etc.) and follow the log-on procedure as you are directed on-screen. The system will direct you to choose a local access number or an 800 number to connect through the modem.

Once you're connected and the main menu screen of your Web browser displays, you'll see a button for accessing the Internet. Click it, and then enter the appropriate Internet address or World Wide Web address in the active field. Or search the Internet by topic or keyword. Go to the **Mail** area of your browser to send and receive e-mail messages. See Chapter 9 for more detail on accessing the Internet and sending and receiving e-mail.

18. Faxing a Document

To send a fax from your laptop, you must connect your modem to a telephone line and configure your software appropriately.

Read your hardware user's manual about connecting your modem to a telephone line. *Refer to your software user's manual* for specific setup and faxing instructions. See Chapter 9 for additional detail.

Connecting the Modem Cable. Your laptop system will have either an internal modem or an optional modem on a PC card. Locate the modem cable that comes with your system. Connect one end of the modem cable into the RJ-11 jack on your computer (this looks like a regular telephone jack). Next, plug the opposite end of the cable into a standard telephone wall jack.

Sending a Fax from Your Laptop. From the Windows 95 **Start** button, point to **Programs** and then point to **Accessories**. Choose **Fax** and then click **Compose New Fax**. Follow the instructions in the **Compose New Fax** wizard (Figure A-14).

Retrieving a Fax Using Windows 95. From the **Start** menu, point to **Programs** and choose **Accessories**. Choose the **Fax** option. Then select **Request a Fax**. The **Request a Fax** wizard pops up. This window allows you to call a fax information service and retrieve a document or file. The wizard guides you through the steps you need to connect to a fax service and download faxes to your laptop (Figure A-15).

Follow the instructions in the **Request a Fax** wizard. After your call is finished, you can double-click on the **Inbox** icon on your **Desktop**. The retrieved fax file will appear there.

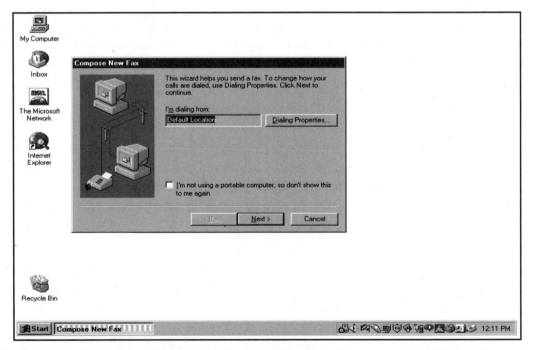

Figure A-14. The **Compose New Fax** wizard on Windows 95 systems will take you through the routine you need to complete for sending a fax.

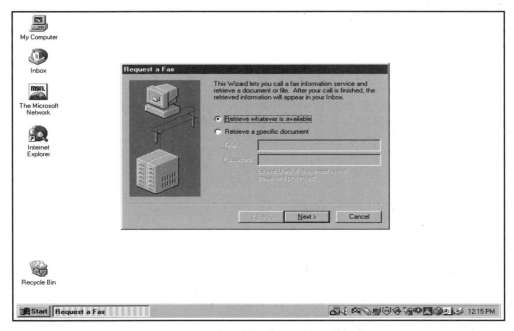

Figure A-15. The **Request a Fax** wizard on Windows 95 will help you connect to a fax service and retrieve faxes.

Faxing a Document	
Windows 98 Instructions	*Windows NT Instructions*
The Windows 98 operating system has removed the fax program that was on Windows 95.	Like Windows 98, Windows NT does not offer a specific fax program, either.
If you have installed Windows 98 over your Windows 95 operating system, the fax function from Windows 95 may have been retained. Try that first.	Use your modem software to fax a document.
	Check your modem user's manual for instructions.
Otherwise, you can still fax a document in Windows 98, but you will do this through your modem software.	Or you can fax from within any Windows application by selecting "fax" as your print option and following the instructions in the dialog box.
Check your modem user's manual for instructions on how to fax from your laptop.	
Or you can fax from within any Windows application by selecting "fax" as your print option and following the instructions in the dialog box.	

19. What to Do If Your System Freezes Up

Freezing up means nothing happens when you click, move the pointing device, or hit any key. If your system freezes up, press [Ctrl] + [Alt] + [Del] simultaneously. This will shut down an unresponsive application. You won't lose any work. To restart, press [Ctrl] + [Alt] + [Del] again.

What to Do If Your System Freezes Up	
Windows 95 and Windows 98 Instructions	*Windows NT Instructions*
First: Try pressing **Esc**. *Second:* Hold **Alt** and press **Enter**. *Last resort:* Press [Ctrl] + [Alt] + [Del]. Click the name of the currently running program. Then click **End Task**. When the system asks whether you're sure, click **Yes**.	*Try this first:* Press **Esc** twice. *Second:* Press [Ctrl] + [Alt] + [Del] all at once. Next, click on the **Task Manager** button, which pops up a list of currently running programs. Click on the offending program. Then click **End Task**. *Third:* Press [Ctrl] + [Alt] + [Del] simultaneously. Then choose **Shut Down**. **Tip:** Avoid the **Reset** button and avoid turning the laptop on and off.

20. Batteries and Power Management

Battery levels and power management are specific to your laptop hardware rather than your software operating system. Consult your laptop user's manual. Each model handles power management a little differently.

Tips

- If you're making a new purchasing decision, buy a laptop with lithium-ion batteries—they last longer.

- In general, use your batteries until they discharge completely before recharging them. This will allow the battery monitor to provide a more accurate charge-level reading. Check your laptop manual.

- Store battery packs in a cool, dry place when they're not in use. High temperatures will cause them to lose their charge more quickly.

- Keep a battery pack in your laptop when you're using it with the plug-in cord to keep it charged up.

- Check your power supply status often by double-clicking the electric plug or battery icon on the **Taskbar**.

- Use your power management utility to preset your computer to **Suspend**, **Hibernate**, or **Shut Down** after a specified time of inactivity.

Some laptops allow you to **Suspend** for more than 100 hours. *Rule of thumb:* If you're not planning to use your laptop for more than 24 hours, save your work and shut down the system completely. Or shut it down every evening, but keep your laptop plugged in to boost battery power to maximum.

21. Shutting Down Your Laptop

Go to the **Start** button and choose **Shut Down**. When the dialog box appears, you'll have a choice to really shut down or to restart. Or you can cancel the request altogether. If you're sure you want to shut down, click **Yes** and wait a moment as the system performs its end routine and shuts down.

Index

About the Authors

Andy Jenkins, Dick Elder, and Dave Thomas are co-owners of TEAM Marketing Group, Inc., a sales training and sales management consulting firm in Englewood, Colorado.

Andy Jenkins is also president of TEAM-CBT, a new division formed to create computer-based training programs and multimedia sales presentations.

Dick Elder is TEAM's president. He has developed and delivered customized training programs for more than 25 years, for some of the world's largest companies, including DuPont, 3M, Eli Lilly, MacGregor Golf, and many others.

Dave Thomas is TEAM's senior consultant. He has more than 25 years of experience in sales management training and corporate sales development. He leads the consulting activities of TEAM.

About TEAM Marketing Group, Inc.

TEAM is a sales training and sales managment consulting firm based in Englewood, Colorado, with a proven track record in helping companies improve their sales and marketing effectiveness. The company's mission is to exceed the expectations of their clients through timely and professional delivery of high-quality, innovative training solutions and sales consulting services. TEAM knows the business of selling.

About *Shoulder-to-Shoulder Selling*

TEAM developed *Shoulder-to-Shoulder Selling,* an off-the-shelf training package, to teach salespeople how to combine salesmanship with the power of a laptop computer to sell more effectively—to get to "yes" faster—during a face-to-face sales call. The package includes a 45-minute instructional videotape, a state-of-the-art CD-ROM, and a copy of *How to Sell with a Laptop.* The program helps salespeople get comfortable with a laptop, prepare for the next sales call, and create dynamic sales presentations. This sales-enhancing kit is packed with tips and techniques for creating excellent presentations and boosting sales success, either one-on-one or in front of a group. For more information on the complete *Shoulder-to-Shoulder Selling* training kit and TEAM Marketing Group, call 1-800-262-6992, or visit their Web site at www.teamdenver.com.